The Senses Still

The Senses Still

Perception and Memory as Material Culture in Modernity

EDITED BY

C. Nadia Seremetakis

THE UNIVERSITY OF CHICAGO PRESS

CHICAGO AND LONDON

Chapter 3 is reprinted, with changes, from *Visualizing Theory: Selected Essays from V.A.R. 1990–1994*, ed. Lucien Taylor (New York: Routledge), 214–229, by permission of the publisher.

The University of Chicago Press, Chicago 60637
The University of Chicago Press, Ltd., London

ISBN 0-226-74877-4 (pbk.)

Library of Congress Cataloging-in-Publication Data

The senses still : perception and memory as material culture in modernity / edited by
C. Nadia Seremetakis.
    p.   cm.
    Originally published: Boulder : Westview Press, 1994.
    Includes bibliographical references.
    1. Material culture.   2. Senses and sensation.   3. Memory.   4. Meaning (Psychol-
ogy)   5. Ethnopsychology.   I. Seremetakis, C. Nadia (Constantina Nadia)
    [GN406.S46   1996]
    155.8—dc20   95-49870
                                                                                  CIP

Contents

Contexts

The contributors to this volume share an interest in the anthropology of everyday life, a frequently ignored crucible for the formation of modern experience. They see everyday sensibilities interacting, in often unacknowledged fashion, with the possibility and truth claims of theoretical discourse. In this case the anthropology of the senses is a central passageway into a self-reflexive epistemology of the modern life-world. The senses in modernity are the switching place where the structure of experience and the structure of knowledge converge and cross.

These themes are deliberately recovered by the authors from the external and internal cultural-historical margins of European and American metropoles. For the construction of modernity can be best witnessed not at the center, which is a perceptual effect, but at the verges; at sites where modernity is an unfinished and contested hegemony. Thus Susan Buck-Morss looks at the perceptual impact of early cinema in revolutionary Soviet Union, Jonas Frykman at the construction of redemptive nature by an embryonic Swedish urbanity, Allen Feldman at the censorship of the pain of racial and ethnic alterities; and I explore the mutual displacement and admixture of both modern and pre-modern sensory memory in the particular developmental circumstances of post–World War II Greece.

The present essays and their methodologies, as much as they are new advances, draw on longstanding research concerns of the contributors. At a quick glance, the contributors have had a common interest in how historical representation and experience are embedded in material culture. They have now turned to perception as a way into the construction of material culture as a historiographic space. Jonas Frykman in his previous studies has been concerned with the social and architectural history of private spaces in Sweden from the 19th century to the present. Susan Buck-Morss opened up new and disconcerting prospects on the perceptual forms of everyday modernity by turning with a renewed vigor and depth to Benjamin's treatment of commodity fetishes as bearers of expelled historical consciousness and utopian hope. Feldman, in his ethnography of the body in Northern Ireland, identified sensory fictions as essential to the material cultures of the state and ethnicity. He treated political violence as a material performance that deposits narratives on

bodies and social space as palpable surfaces of historical depiction. Paul
Stoller, in contemporary African contexts, identified the blindness and
insight that can emerge from the confusion of incommensurate sensory
systems. He has listened to the silent dialogues that occur between persons and substances in the ethnographic process of knowing. Stoller recently expanded the concept of ethnographic self-reflexivity beyond text-
centered models and into visual communication in his study of Jean
Rouch. My ethnography of women's resistance and material culture in
rural and urban Greece was concerned with the inseparability of the
senses and emotions and with the ways a gendered historical consciousness is both emotionally and poetically stored in material culture and
mourning rituals. The essays in this book originate in part from a panel I
organized at the 1991 meetings of the American Anthropological Association, titled "The Anthropology of the Senses and European Modernity."
Since then the scope and subject matter of some of the essays have
changed but the basic concerns of the 1991 panel remain. Paul Stoller was
the discussant in the 1991 panel, which also featured the poet Olga Brou-
mas. In his essay in this volume, he comments on the different articles,
which I also discuss extensively in the last chapter.

*   *   *

This discussion of the senses had its personal origins in my cross-cultural
everyday and teaching experiences in two continents, which have divided
my life the past eighteen years. At New York University, for instance, in
my seminars, linguistic terms such as nostalgia (discussed later in my
essays), when used by students of Greek background, became entries
into sensory difference and pointed to the pertinence of etymological archaeology. Since nostalgia derives from Greek, these students assumed
that the Greek meaning was transported intact into the American context. The resulting cross-cultural non-communication was as shocking to
them as any first encounter in the field. At the University of Crete (where
I was invited to introduce anthropology in 1990–92, during my most recent field research in Greece), the theme of the senses in the context of
everyday experiences, and my emphasis on the perceptual "detail," often
unnoticed by conventional sociological and philosophical optics, was described by the students as an "awakening." Everyday expressions such
as "I hear the garlic" (referring to its taste) transformed the classroom into a
fieldsite. Students from Crete and the Peloponnese, for instance, took the
expression for granted, but Athenians did not know it. The materialization
of regional multiplicity, of the heterogeneity of Greek culture right there and
then, brought anthropology home. And it left me with the nagging question: What are the conditions of anthropology's possibility in a European
periphery, and what form and content should it take in such contexts?

The turn to everyday life as a pedagogical, historical, and cultural resource at that moment in Greek society was apt. Generic discourses on "loss" and social crises, which have long characterized the languages of the state, politicians, and popular media, as well as social scientists, had recently been intensified. This fixation on loss and crisis turns the self-irony, self-reflexivity, of Greek culture into a destructive, paralyzing, numbing exercise. The discourse on loss, which offers no alternatives, empties the neo-colonial site of all internal content, leaving it an empty and receptive shell for external cultural colonization. Thus the ideologies of loss and crisis in the neo-colonial periphery are an integral part of the political logic of mimetic modernization. (The discourse on loss, in the context of an anthropology of the senses, is discussed in the last chapter.) The narratives of loss are in turn complemented by their extreme opposite: suspicion and xenophobia towards anything different. Any perspective therefore that speaks to the semantic and historical resources in the unacknowledged depths of everyday life and language *and* to internal cultural and historical heterogeneity is bound to be contentious in such a political climate of social abjection.

On a short visit back to New York during that time, and while planning the 1991 panel, I met with Susan Buck-Morss. Between sips of Greek brandy we talked of her own experiences in Crete, where she had spent quite some time early in her career. She had been invited to offer a lecture once at the university there: "I first spoke on tourism and its effects on everyday life in Crete, and I got the sense I perplexed them, as if I took them to another world. What was an Adorno theorist doing with tourism in Crete? But once I began speaking of Adorno . . ." "They felt at home!" I interjected, and we burst out laughing.

The defacement of everyday life and the ritual crisis provoked by the discourse of loss must be seen as neo-colonial adaptations to an arbitrary modernity that is staged not only in Greece but in other peripheries both inside and outside of Europe. For anthropology this carries a particular salience. In Eastern and Southern European countries, anthropological frameworks and methodologies are being imported as finished and frequently closed systems of knowledge, although they are settled on top of complex cultural and political environments. In Greece, British structural functionalism on one side and the American "new ethnography" perspectives[1] on the other are imitated by "young" anthropologists in a rather rote fashion. The circumstances of their reception recalls the style of learning promoted by Greek educational institutions, that is, passive memorization, mechanical internalization of external content, an epistemological process that bypasses students' own internal content. Such mimetic dynamics now reappear in the Greek reception of the various schools of anthropology. The latter are being mediated by neo-colonial subtexts ignored by both the Greek respondents and the British and American brokers of these frameworks. Another example is the recent proliferation of studies on commensality by European anthropologists (as evidenced also in the first conference of The European Association of Social Anthropologists in 1990). The new interest in food-ways is a programmatic response to the availability of EEC funds for the study of nutrition. This ethnographic research agenda is now a component of the EEC's rationalization and centralization of food production and consumption policies.

The pertinence of the anthropology of the senses lies in the fact that long standing and often hidden sensory-perceptual dispositions are imported in and along with these ethnographic perspectives; they should be critically examined in their new recontextualization in other cultures. What zones of admissible and inadmissible experience and ethnographic perception are being established when British and American—and to a lesser degree French—theoretical frameworks, for instance, are exported wholesale as seductive capital to cultural peripheries that are struggling to move from object to subject status in the world-systems of discourse and knowledge?

This volume attempts to show that anthropology and social history are not finished systems of knowledge that can be holistically taught and disseminated in other cultural sites. Rather, any recontextualization of anthropological discourse and method should open them up to fundamental questioning from the perspective of the senses among possible others. This has been exactly my experience in teaching anthropology and gender in Greek contexts and elsewhere. It is from my personal re-contextualization that the problematic of the senses emerged for me; and in this case, the senses spoke to a need to develop a "native anthropology" that would be genuinely cross-cultural, in both directions, for it would examine, analyze and reframe the inevitable neo-colonial mimesis that emerges when knowledge systems that lack parity meet.

*   *   *

Neither the 1991 panel nor my particular approach to the senses in this volume (and earlier in *The Last Word*) would have come about without the long and ongoing dialogues, voiced and silent, with my students in both continents; with numerous friends in Greece, especially Elpida and Evridiki; with all those scholars whose foundational works I discuss in this text; and, most of all, with my friend and colleague Allen Feldman whose generous mind has carefully listened to my concerns and anxieties about the state of anthropology in European peripheries far too long. My essay in Chapter 3, in particular, has benefited from old and recent comments on different occasions from Paul Stoller, Lucien Taylor, Fred Myers, Michael Taussig, and the faculty of the department of anthropology of the University of Chicago, where it was also presented in 1992.

C. Nadia Seremetakis
New York 1992

Notes

1. Ethnological and ethnographic concepts have recently been brokered into Greek university culture. The indigenous comprehension of anthropological perspectives is mediated, if not distorted, by *how* these have entered contemporary Greek thought and *who* has effected that entry.

Thus, various schools of anthropological theory and method do not only operate as bodies of knowledge but also function as exclusionary gate-keepers of the study, teaching, research, and discourse of anthropology itself. There are basically two gates one must pass in order to gain access to the discourse of anthropology in Greece: a school of British structural functionalism and its related publications that unproblematically constructs anthropology as an unambiguous scientific body of knowledge, and which issues forth overarching generalizations of Greek life that have their origins in long outdated Africanist models of kinship; and an equally scientific sociology-policy studies department that flirts with applied anthropology and EEC money, and which has also turned to the American "new ethnography" to the extent that the latter can be conveniently misread as inherently anti-ethnographic.

Thus, highly truncated theoretical surveys of ethnological and ethnographic theory are rapidly mobilized and disseminated in a formulaic fashion to meet the demands of faculty, students, and other departments to set and fix a canon. These incomplete renderings of a complex theoretical history and highly diverse body of knowledge never account for the trans-cultural intervention implied by the very insertion of anthropological discourse in the current Greek context. Of course, the socio-cultural and historico-political contexts in which the various emulated discourses developed are flatly ignored as is the current context in which they are received; and in this fashion, concerned Greeks evade and deny their own prior and current object status in the Western European human sciences which dates back to the 19th century.

Here traditional Greek educational formalism, which promotes the rote learning of fixed bodies of knowledge, has combined with a neocolonial mimicry and commodification of an exotic, yet progressive, Western Other, in a manner that replicates the peripheral positioning of Greek cultural production in relation to various societies of the Euro-American metropole. *Anthropology, the very discipline that was supposed to examine such phenomena, becomes the highest expression and emblematic means of cultural colonization.* The anthropology of Greece in Greece is whittled down and compressed to fit an existing narrow social consciousness of the Other that is partly dictated by that Other. Thus the British and American theorists (and to a lesser degree French theorists) who have aided and abetted the dissemination of anthropological factionalism reveal minimal sensitivity of their transformative impact on the cultural context that is the object of their technical assistance and ideological transfer. This combined with the development of a reified, ahistorical iconography of Euro-American ethnological theory has resulted in a novel and ongoing rationalization of modern Greek culture. It is this symbiotic rationalization of culture and the facilitating practices of the university, the conference, and the canonical syllabus that should be the necessary and proper object of critical ethnographic analysis, *since the business of making "Greek culture" is now under the institutional monopoly of those whose mission was to study it.*

1

The Memory of the Senses, Part I: Marks of the Transitory

C. Nadia Seremetakis

The Breast of Aphrodite

I grew up with the peach. It had a thin skin touched with fuzz, and a soft matte off-white color alternating with rosy hues. *Rodhákino* was its name (*ródho* means rose). It was well rounded and smooth like a small clay vase, fitting perfectly into your palm. Its interior was firm yet moist, offering a soft resistance to the teeth. A bit sweet and a bit sour, it exuded a distinct fragrance. This peach was known as "the breast of Aphrodite" (*o mastós tis Afrodhítis*).

A relation of this peach appeared eventually in the markets, which was called *yermás*. It was a much softer, watery fruit with a yolkish yellow color and reddish patches. Its silky thin skin would slide off at a touch revealing its slippery, shiny, deep yellow interior that melted with no resistance in the mouth. Both fruits were very sensitive, easy to bruise. I learned to like them both but my heart was set for the *rodhákino*.

In the United States, all fruits resembling either the *rodhákino* or *yermás* are named "peach." Throughout my years in the States, the memory of my peach was in its difference.

Every journey back was marked by its taste. Summer was its permanent referent, yet its gradual disappearance from the summer markets passed almost unnoticed. A few years ago, I realized that the peach was nowhere to be found in the markets, in or outside of Athens. When I mentioned it in casual conversations to friends and relatives, they responded as if the peach is always out there although they did not happen to eat it lately. What they are mainly buying, they explained, is a kind of *yermadho-rodhákino* (a blend of *yermás* and *rodhákino*). People only alluded to the disappearance of the older peach by remarking on the tastelessness of new varieties, a comment that was often extended to all food, "nothing tastes as good as the past."

As my search for the peach became more persistent, my disappoint-
ment matched their surprise in the realization that the peach was gone
forever. I asked my father to plant it in our fields in the country to rescue
it, but he has yet to find it. My older friends began to bring me tokens
from their neighborhood markets, as well as from the country whenever
they traveled out of the city. We all agreed that there were varieties that
carried one or two of the characteristics of "our peach" but they were far
from it. The part had taken the name of the whole.

In the presence of all those "peaches," the absent peach became narrative. It was as if when something leaves, it only goes externally, for its
body persists within persons. The peach was its memory, and as if both
had gone underground, they waited to be named. My naming of its absence resurrected observations, commentaries, stories, some of which encapsulated whole epochs marked by their own sensibilities. "Ah, that
peach, what an aroma! and taste! The breast of Aphrodite we called it.
These (peaches and other food) today have no taste (á-nosta)."

The younger generation, whenever present, heard these stories as if
listening to a captivating fairy tale. For me the peach had been both eaten
and remembered, but for the younger generation it was now digested
through memory and language. At the same time, we are all experiencing
the introduction from foreign markets of new fruits with no Greek prece-
dents, such as the kiwi. For the younger generation, the remembered first
peach exists on the same exotic plane as the kiwi. For the generation that
follows, the kiwi, no longer exotic, may evoke a different sensibility.

The disappearance of Aphrodite's peach is a double absence; it reveals
the extent to which the senses are entangled with history, memory, forgetfulness, narrative and silence. That first peach of my childhood carried with it allusions to distant epochs where the relation between food
and the erotic was perhaps more explicit, named, and sacrilized; a relation that although fragmented and gone underground, was carried over
through the centuries by the *rodhákino*, a fruit bearing myth in its form.

The new fruits displaced the *rodhákino* and together with it, a mosaic
of enmeshed memories, tastes, aromas. The surrogate remains as a simulation with no model, emptied of specific cultural content and actively
producing forgetfulness. A shift has been accomplished from sedimented
depth to surface with no past. Aphrodite's peach in its presence and later
absence materialized experiences of time which are searched for fruit-
lessly in the peach of today. This complicity of history and the senses also
refers to the relation between *Eros* and *Thanatos* where the latter is not
mere absence or void but rather material closure, a cordoning off of the
capacity for certain perceptual experiences in such a manner that their
very disappearance goes unnoticed.

How are the transformations of the senses experienced and conceptu-
alized? This is also to ask, how is history experienced and thought of, on

the level of the everyday? What elements in a culture enable the sensory experience of history? Where can historicity be found? in what sensory forms and practices? And to what extent the experience of and the capacity to narrate history is tied to the senses? Is memory stored in specific everyday items that form the historicity of a culture, items that create and sustain our relationship to the historical as a sensory dimension?

*   *   *

Is the disappearance of Aphrodite's peach an idiosyncratic event? Or does the disappearance of the "particular" peach as micro-history materialize on the everyday sweeping, macro-historical, sociocultural changes? The vanishing of tastes, aromas, and textures are being writ large in contemporary European margins with the joint expansion and centralizations of EEC market rationalities. The erasure of one Greek peach poses the question: at what experiential levels are the economic and social transformations of the EEC being felt? Under the rationale of trans-national uniformity the EEC may have initiated a massive intervention in the commensal cultures of its membership by determining what regional varieties of basic food staples can be grown, marketed and exported. Certain types of Irish potatoes, German beer, and French cheese are no longer admissible into the public market, no longer eligible for subsidies because they look, appear, and taste different, and in some cases violate new health regulations.

In Greece, as regional products gradually disappear, they are replaced by foreign foods, foreign tastes; the universal and rationalized is now imported into the European periphery as the exotic. Here a regional diversity is substituted by a surplus over-production. This EEC project implicitly constitutes a massive resocialization of existing consumer cultures and sensibilities, as well as a reorganization of public memory. A French cheese is excluded because it is produced through a specific fermentation process; one that market regulations deem a health-risk. What is fermentation if not history? If not a maturation that occurs through the articulation of time and substance? Sensory premises, memories and histories are being pulled out from under entire regional cultures and the capacity to reproduce social identities may be altered as a result. Such economic processes reveal the extent to which the ability to replicate cultural identity is a material practice embedded in the reciprocities, aesthetics, and sensory strata of material objects. Sensory displacement does not only relate to cultures of consumption but to those local material cultures of production where the latter is still symbolically mediated and not yet reduced to a purely instrumental practice. Sensory changes occur microscopically through everyday accretion; so, that which shifts the material culture of perception is itself imperceptible and only reappears after the fact in fairy tales, myths, and memories that hover at the margins of speech.

The imperceptible is not only the consequence of sensory transformation but also the means by which it takes place. Thus the problematic of the senses in modernity resurrects the old theme ignored in recent anthropological theory, that of the historical unconscious.

The Impeachment of Nostalgia

The memory of Aphrodite's peach is nostalgic. What is the relation of nostalgia to the senses and history? In English the word nostalgia (in Greek *nostalghía*) implies trivializing romantic sentimentality. In Greek the verb *nostalghó* is a composite of *nostó* and *alghó*. *Nostó* means I return, I travel (back to homeland); the noun *nóstos* means the return, the journey, while *á-nostos* means without taste, as the new peaches are described (*ánosta*, in plural). The opposite of *ánostos* is *nóstimos* and characterizes someone or something that has journeyed and arrived, has matured, ripened and is thus tasty (and useful). *Alghó* means I feel pain, I ache for, and the noun *álghos* characterizes one's pain in soul and body, burning pain (*kaimós*). Thus *nostalghía* is the desire or longing with burning pain to journey. It also evokes the sensory dimension of memory in exile and estrangement; it mixes bodily and emotional pain and ties painful experiences of spiritual and somatic exile to the notion of maturation and ripening. In this sense, *nostalghía* is linked to the personal consequences of historicizing sensory experience which is conceived as a painful bodily and emotional journey.

Nostalghía thus is far from trivializing romantic sentimentality. This reduction of the term confines the past and removes it from any transactional and material relation to the present; the past becomes an isolatable and consumable unit of time. Nostalgia, in the American sense, freezes the past in such a manner as to preclude it from any capacity for social transformation in the present, preventing the present from establishing a dynamic perceptual relationship to its history. Whereas the Greek etymology evokes the transformative impact of the past as unreconciled historical experience.[1] Does the difference between nostalgia and *nostalghía* speak of different cultural experiences of the senses and memory? Could a dialogical encounter of the terms offer insights for an anthropology of the senses?

Sensory Exchange and Performance

Nostalghía speaks to the sensory reception of history. In Greek there is a semantic circuit that weds the sensorial to agency, memory, finitude, and therefore history—all of which are contained within the etymological strata of the senses. The word for senses is *aesthísis;* emotion-feeling and aesthetics are respectively *aésthima* and *aesthitikí*. They all derive from the verb *aesthánome* or *aesthísome* meaning I feel or sense, I understand, grasp, learn or receive news or information, and I have an accurate sense of good and evil, that is I judge correctly. *Aesthísis* is defined as action or power through the medium of the senses, and the media or the *semía* (points, tracks, marks) by which one senses. *Aésthima*, emotion feeling, is also an ailment of the soul, an event that happens, that impacts on one viscerally through the senses; it also refers to romance, love affair. A strong *aésthima* is called *páthos* (passion). This includes the sense of suffering, illness, but also the English sense of passion, as in "he has a passion for music." The stem verb *pathéno* means I provoke passion in both its meanings; I am acting, moving by an internal forceful *aésthima*, passion; I get inspired, excited; I suffer. Among Greek youth the word *pathéno* as in "when I hear this song *pathéno*," is common. The gestures accompanying it, such as hitting and holding the forehead, and the matching sounds, express both (sudden) suffering and extreme enjoyment.

A synonym of *pathéno* in this case is *pethéno*, I die. *Páthos* (passion) is the meeting point of *éros* and *thánatos;* where the latter is an internal death, the death of the self because of and for the other; the moment that the self is both the self and a memory in the other. Death is a journey; a sensorial journey into the other. So is *éros*. The common expression during love making is *me péthanes* (you made me die, I died because of, for you and through you). *Éros* is desire. It also means appetite. The expression often used in vernacular Greek, e.g., from mother to child, to show extreme desire is "I'll eat you." The same expression is used for someone causing suffering, e.g., child to parent, "you ate me." In the journey of death, to the otherworld, the earth "eats" the body.

In these semantic currents we find no clear cut boundaries between the senses and emotions, the mind and body, pleasure and pain, the voluntary and the involuntary, and affective and aesthetic experience. Such culturally specific perspectives on sensory experience are not sheer comparative curiosities. They are crucial for opening up a self reflexive, culturally and historically informed consideration of the senses. Sensory semantics in Greek culture, among others, contain regional epistemologies, in-built theories, that provoke important cross-cultural methodological consequences.

* * *

The senses represent inner states not shown on the surface. They are also located in a social-material field outside of the body. Consider the Greek expression "his eyes witness fear" (*ta mátia tou martyráne fóvo*) and the English gloss "his eyes show fear." The latter speaks of fear as an inner psychological state, while "his eyes witness fear" can speak of fear as if it is out there, external to and autonomous of the body, and involuntarily marked on the senses. Here the sense organs become tracks, *semía*, where fear is received by the body. The sense organs function in the same manner that the material artifact can also function, that is as *semíon*, track, which one senses and a medium by which one senses. Thus the sensory is not only encapsulated within the body as an internal capacity or power, but is also dispersed out there on the surface of things as the latter's autonomous characteristics, which then can invade the body as perceptual experience. Here sensory interiors and exteriors constantly pass into each other in the creation of extra-personal significance.

A related saying, "his eyes witnessed him" or "betrayed him," and "I saw it in his eyes" (despite his talk), speaks of the involuntary aspect of sensory experience which discloses inner states not intended by the subject. Thus although "his speech" may have attempted to lie, "his eyes revealed the truth" *to my eyes*. The sense organs can exchange with each other. The senses are meaning-generating apparatuses that operate beyond consciousness and intention. The interpretation of and through the senses becomes a recovery of truth as collective, material experience.

The senses are also implicated in historical interpretation as witnesses or record-keepers of material experience. There is an autonomous circuit beween inner and outer sensory states and fields, that constitutes an independent sphere of perceptual exchange and reciprocity. The senses, like language, are a social fact to the extent that they are a collective medium of communication that is both voluntary and involuntary, stylized and personal. For example, the Greek term for perception is *antílipsi* (*lípsi* means reception, while the prefix *antí* refers to equivalence, reciprocity, face to face, in place of and not only opposition as in English). *Antílipsi* is thus defined as the act of receiving in an exchange.

There is a corporate communication between the body and things, the person and the world, which points to the perceptual construction of truth as the involuntary disclosure of meaning through the senses. Although the senses are a social and collective institution like language, they *are not* reducible to language. Thus sensory meaning as truth, in Greece, introduces an ironic counterpoint to any linguistic discourse. What is being said may be relativized, contradicted or confirmed by embodied acts, gestures, and sensory affects. This process of confirmation or negation is a performative moment where gestures and/or a surround of artifacts are mobilized to bear or deny witness to language. Truth therefore is extra-linguistic and revealed through expression, performance, material culture and conditions of embodiment.

The involuntary circuit of the senses reveals that embodied performance is in part constructed out of the cross-communication of senses and things. This speaks of a social aesthetics that is not purely a contracted or negotiated synchrony but one that is embedded in, and inherited from, an autonomous network of object relations and prior sensory exchanges. Performance therefore is elicited by externality and history as much as it may come from within.

The sensory landscape and its meaning-endowed objects bear within them emotional and historical sedimentation that can provoke and ignite gestures, discourses and acts—acts which open up these objects' stratigraphy. Thus the surround of material culture is neither stable nor fixed, but inherently transitive, demanding connection and completion by the perceiver. Performance can be such an act of perceptual completion as opposed to being a manipulative theatrical display.[2] Performance is also a moment where the unconscious levels and accumulated layers of personal experience become conscious through material networks, independent of the performer. However, the mode and content of completion/connection with the sensory artifact is not determined in advance, it is not a communication with a Platonic essense, but rather it is a mutation of meaning and memory that refracts the mutual insertion of the perceiver and perceived in historical experience and possibly their mutual alienation from public culture, offical memory and formal economies. This *performance is not "performative"*—the instantiation of a pre-existing code. It is a *poesis*, the making of something out of that which was previously experientially and culturally unmarked or even null and void. Here sensory memory, as the meditation on the historical substance of experience is not mere repetition but transformation which brings the past into the present as a natal event. In this moment the actor is also the audience of his/her involuntary implication in a sensory horizon. This can be a moment of sensory self-reflexivity and because it is located within, and generated by, material forces, we can begin to see how material culture functions as an apparatus for the production of *social and historical reflexivity*.

Sour Grapes

Not only have some foreign fruits arrived in Greek markets—it is no coincidence that in colloquial Greek a strange or weird person is referred to as "a strange fruit" or "a new fruit"—but also familiar fruits have made their timid appearance in fancy supermarkets at the "wrong season." For instance grapes, emblematic of the summer for Greeks, appeared in the winter under the sign "imported from EEC." Observing local women shopping, touching, picking and choosing, one notices that they pass them over as if they never noticed them, or commenting on how "sour they look." Sour implies not yet ripened, thus not in season, and so tasteless (*ánosta*). And while the EEC in this case becomes identified with sour grapes, a whole epoch, the present, is characterized as *ánosto*.

When and how does an epoch, a slice of history, become something *ánosto*? To say that aspects of daily life have become tasteless, to make parts substitute for the whole, implies that the capacity to synthesize perceptual experience, is only accessible through dispersed fragments. The movement from real or imagined wholes to parts and fragments is a metaphorical slide that captures the movement of history through a shifting perceptual focus. The capacity to replicate a sensorial culture resides in a dynamic interaction between perception, memory and a landscape of artifacts, organic and inorganic. This capacity can atrophy when that landscape, as a repository and horizon of historical experience, emotions, embedded sensibilities and hence social identities, disolves into disconnected pieces. At the same time, what replaces it?

When new forms and items of an emerging material culture step in-between a society's present perceptual existence and its residual sociocultural identity, they can be tasteless because people may no longer have the perceptual means for seeking identity and experience in new material forms. Because the cultural instruments for creating meaning out of material experience have been dispersed with the now discarded past sensory landscape. The latter was didactic as much as it was an object of perception and utility. The characterization *ánosto* (tasteless) then deals with the cultural incapacity to codify past, present,and anticipatory experiences at the level of sensory existence. This is so because such codifying practices are never purely mentalist but embedded in and borne by a material world of talking objects.

This is why the enthusiastic reception of the "new" is imported, culturally prepared and programmed with the simultaneous fabrication or promise of new sensory powers—the latter are automatically bonded with the items of the penetrating culture. Thus each commodity form is introduced through the creation of its own self-generating experience and memory. The latter are themselves promised as substitutions, replacements and improvements of prior sensory experience.

In cultures that undergo colonial and post-colonial experiences of transformation, the experience of tastelessness can be self-imposed for they have internalized "the eye of the Other" (Seremetakis 1984) and see their own culture and residual experience from a position of defamiliarization and estrangement. This can result in a newly constructed archaicization of recent and unreconcilable experiences, practices, and narratives. Particular and now idiocyncratic cultural experiences are described as having long disappeared, as lost, when in fact they are quite recent and their memory sharp. As one moves deeper into conversation with people, their intimacy with these distant practices comes out as fairy tales, anecdotes, folklore, and myth. The historical repression of memory that the cultural periphery can impose on itself is as rapid, shallow, profound and experientially painful as any other disorienting penetration of metropolitan modernity. The discourse on loss is an element of public culture, an official ideological stance taken towards the past that aligns the speaker with the normative view of the present, i.e., modern times. Yet as the discourse of loss congeals into an element of public culture, that which has never been lost, but which can no longer be said, shared and exchanged, becomes the content of unreconciled personal and privatized experience.[3]

Sensory and Historical Multiplicity

What can be lost is not the senses but the memory of the senses. The erasure of this memory renders the senses as imperceptible as the passing of Aphrodite's peach. There is no such thing as one moment of perception and then another of memory, representation or objectification. Mnemonic processes are intertwined with the sensory order in such a manner as to render each perception a re-perception. Re-perception is the creation of meaning through the interplay, witnessing, and cross-metaphorization of co-implicated sensory spheres. Memory cannot be confined to a purely mentalist or subjective sphere. It is a culturally mediated material practice that is activated by embodied acts and semantically dense objects. This material approach to memory places the senses in time and speaks to memory as both meta-sensory capacity and as a sense organ in-it-self.

Memory as a distinct meta-sense transports, bridges and crosses all the other senses. Yet memory is internal to each sense, and the senses are as divisible and indivisible from each other as each memory is separable and intertwined with others. Memory is the horizon of sensory experiences, storing and restoring the experience of each sensory dimension in another, as well as dispersing and finding sensory records outside the body in a surround of entangling objects and places. Memory and the senses are co-mingled in so far as they are equally involuntary experiences. Their involuntary dimension points to their encompassment by a trans-individual social and somatic landscape.

* * *

The particular effacement of sensory memory in modernity, is mainly a consequence of an extreme division of labor, perceptual specialization and rationalization. The senses, in modernity, are detached from each other, re-functioned and externalized as utilitarian instruments, and as media and objects of commodification. The carving out and partitioning of separate domains of perceptual acquisition also authorizes the sheer literality of sensory experience. The literal is a symbolic logic produced by the scientific rationalization of the senses and/or by a culture of specialized consumption. The result is the privatized sense organ (see Jameson 1981; Harvey 1989; Crary 1991). The literality of the thing, as its most digestible and commodifiable dimension, allows hyper-consumption. Literality, as a cultural code, prescribes and insures norms of limited, functional and repetitious engagement with the disposable commodity unit. The paradox is that, in the repeated performance of consumption, the commodity form, despite its episodic character and the ongoing obsolence of the new, is elaborated as the dominant perceptual logic of things. In the high turn-over of commodity experiences, each object, each material experience, is the absence of the other and the sensory investment it provoked. Each episode of consumption is relatively absolute and quickly totalizing because it never lingers long enough in the senses as social memory to be stitched into a historical fabric with the others it has displaced.

As Ernst Bloch (1991), Walter Benjamin (1969, 1973, 1978) and the Surrealists insisted, the cosmos of economically discarded cultural artifacts constitutes a vast social unconscious of sensory-emotive experience that potentially offers up hidden and now inadmissible counter-narratives of once valued lifeworlds. These critics pitted the latent utopian sensibility, locked within the disfunctional and the useless, against the functional, utilitarian and compulsory wastage of a political culture of fashion. Benjamin, Bloch, the artist Max Ernst, as chroniclers of the first encounter with late modernity, recovered utopian feeling, alterity and cultural procreation in the lost, negated, de-commodified attics and basements of everyday life.   It was in these sites that they relocated social memory as a sphere that tripped-up the closures of public memory, official histories and the idea of progress. Within this framework, the article invested with surplus memory and meanings becomes a separate and distinct(monadic) memory-form in-it-self; it carries within it the sensorial off-print of its human use and triggered desires; when it is discarded and rendered inaudible, an entire anthropology is thrown away with it.

*   *   *

Mnemonic sensory experience implies that the artifact bears within it layered commensal meanings (shared substance and material reciprocities), and histories. It can also be an instrument for mobilizing the perceptual penetration of historical matter. As a sensory form in itself, the artifact can provoke the emergence, the awakening of the layered memories, and thus the senses contained within it. The object invested with sensory memory speaks; it provokes re-call as a missing, detached yet antiphonic element of the perceiver. The sensory connection between perceiver and artifact completes the latter in an unexpected and nonprescribed fashion because the perceiver is also the recipient of the unintended historical after-effects of the artifact's presence *or* absence.

Commensal events devoted to the consumption, distribution, sharing and exchange of substances, are usually seen as performances and protocols whose synchronic rules and structure are kept in people's heads like a pre-programmed game plan (as in Douglas 1991). Instead, I have been suggesting that the artifact laden with perceptual recall, is a temporal conduit within which commensal histories and perceptual topographies are borne through time and space, and in a manner that often runs counter to the official cultural codes for the disposition of things. Thus not any object or substance can acquire meaning and value by simply being inserted into rules, times and spaces of commensality which "permit" it to be consumed, shared, exchanged and enjoyed. Rather, artifacts are in themselves histories of prior commensal events and emotional sensory exchanges, and it is these very histories that are exchanged at commensal events and that qualify the object as commensal in the first place. At the same time, the historicity of the commensal artifact can be effaced, forgotten or denied by current cultural, economic and commensal codes. Recovery of the artifact's commensal depth, in this context, reanimates alternative codes and other relations of shared experiential substance.

This approach shows the extent to which the senses are embodied in objects that can provide a multiplicity of possible and always autonomous prospects on their human authors (authorship is not only linked to production but also to use and consumption as identity-conferring performances). Artifacts as memory forms cannot only be viewed from the perspective of their sanctioned use and literal functions. The latter mainly respond to the pre-set cultural limits of specific conditions of production and overtly prescribed modes of consumption. The artifact as the bearer of sensory multiplicity is a catchment zone of perceptions, a lens through which the senses can be explored from their other side: matter as both the terminus of human actions and the carrier of surplus meanings of those actions. Thus it is an unrecognized double of the human body. Between the body and its non-identical doubles, the senses exist in transit, as multi-directional channels of meaning whether one moves from person to person, thing to thing, person to thing, or thing to person.

*   *   *

The memory of the senses speaks to a *reception theory of material culture*, from both the different perspectives of interacting, perceiving subjects and that of the perceptible talking object (formed from a constellation of human acts). Meaning-endowed objects constitute indigenous, regional nets of sensory receipt. Sediments of sensory memory stratify the artifact as depth, forming a diachronic volume, from which all historical matter, valued and devalued, may seep as expressive material culture. The memory of the senses runs against the socio-economic currents that treat artifacts and personal material experiences as dust. *Dust* is created by any perceptual stance that hastily traverses the object world, skims over its surface, treating it as a nullity that casts no meaning into our bodies, or recovers no stories from our past.

Stillness

Articles invested with sensory memory, with regional narratives, are frequently non-synchronous; they are out of the immediate continuum of socially constructed material presence and value. They drag the after-effects of recent, yet now inadmissible social experience. Society does not change all at once or in one piece. And dominant cultural codes are not the only inheritance that we transmit to ourselves and to others who come after. Social transformation is uneven. And it is this unevenness, the non-contemporaneity of the social formation with it-self, that pre-serves and produces non-synchronous, interruptive articles, spaces, acts and narratives. These can stand like a dark stone against the onward rush and transparency of ahistorical time and part the encompassing and mythic seamless present. There are expressions of non-synchronicity which become material encounters with cultural absence and possibility. There are islands of historicity, discontinuous punctures, that render the imperceptible perceptible as they produce marked moments—tidal pools where an experiential cosmos can be mapped out in miniature.

These islands may emancipate sensory experience from the social structure of silence. The artifacts as memory-forms are passageways into the autonomous entanglements of everyday material experience. They can halt the customary unfolding of everyday life by generating other languages against the blanketing of commonsensical codes that rational-ize the skimmed experience of the everyday as totality.

Against the flow of the present, there is a stillness in the material cul-ture of historicity; those things, spaces, gestures, and tales that signify the perceptual capacity for elemental historical creation. *Stillness* is the mo-ment when the buried, the discarded, and the forgotten escape to the social surface of awareness like life-supporting oxygen. It is the moment of exit from historical dust.

What was previously imperceptible and now became "real" was in fact always there as an element of the material culture of the unconscious. The imperceptible has a social structure based on culturally pre-scribed zones of non-experience and canceled meaning. At this juncture, a politics of the senses is brought into play. Everyday life is always a priv-ileged site of political colonization because the everyday, prepared as a zone of devaluation, forgetfullness, and inattention, is also the site where new political identities can be fabricated by techniques of distraction; where power can make its own self-referential histories by absenting any thing that relativizes it. Everyday life is mythicized as the atopic and as the repository of passivity precisely because it harbors the most elusive depths, obscure corners, transient corridors that evade political grids and controls. Yet everyday life is also the zone of lost glances, oblique views and angles where micro-practices leak through the crevices and cracks of official cultures and memories.

Monads and Nomads

There are substances, spaces and times that can trigger stillness. I think of the old Greek who halted from his daily activity in the heat of the mid-day to slowly sip his coffee, each sip followed by a sigh of release. This was a "resting point," a moment of contemplation, the moment he began to re-taste the day. Introduced by aroma and taste, this was a mo-ment of stillness. Each sip and sigh signaling a deepening in thought, re-turning "*logismós* (thought) to distant times." Coffee is *sintrofiá* (friendly companion), as the saying goes. *Sintrofiá* generates a moment of meta-commentary in which the entire scenography of present and past social landscapes are arrayed before his consciousness: the contemporary polit-ical situation, familial events, village circumstances, the weather, crops, international news, all mixed together. There is a perceptual compression of space and time that is encapsulated in the small coffee cup, from which he takes a sip every other minute, and while feeling the sediments on his tongue, he makes his passage through this diversity.

This is the moment that he will think and express, alone or with other drinkers, his *parápono*, a meta-commentary, as an exchange and sharing, of the cycle of pains, emotions, and joys of everyday life. *Parápono* is the narrative of everyday life. It is not a complaint in the English sense of the term, for it does not necessarily require redress or rectification. It can be a sheer presentation of the substance of everyday experience which resists resolution, defies any sense of an ending. *Parápono* (*pónos* means pain) can be but the establishment of the truthfulness of that experience, and for that to happen he needs a *sintrofiá*. It is worth pausing to listen to the etymology of the word. It derives from the verb *tréfo* meaning I feed, raise, cultivate (dreams, ideas, hopes). *Sin-tréfo* (-ome), composed of the prefix *sin* (co-) and *tréfo*, means I feed (I am fed) together with, I solidify, congeal, unify. *Sintrofiá* in colloquial Greek refers to a group of friends, a close companion (human or non-human).

The generic experiences of everyday life transmuted into the aroma and taste of the coffee are sipped along with it. *Ton pótise pharmáki*, "watering someone with poison (pain or negative experience)" or "with joy," is a saying that captures the body's saturation of everyday experience as substance. In popular songs we also hear the expression "I will drink you sip by sip" which evokes a slow maturation of a human relationship, a duration that brings into play the senses and memory. When something is good or beautiful, one desires to "drink it from a glass" (*na to piís sto potíri*). The experience that embodies sensory, emotional engagement and remembrance is received in an encapsulated form; shifted from its origin into a surrogate container, a storage vehicle, a substance from which it can be released, liberated at moments of stillness. Encapsulation forms the plurality of the unnarrativized, taken for granted, and imperceptible into a meta-narrative. The meta-narrative is perceived or spoken as a slowing down of "normal" temporal passage. This decompression of routine temporal experience and its subsequent re-compression into surrogate vehicle and substance is not a stop. It is a different movement within time that captures everyday temporal experience from another oblique angle as if the sensory array is shifted from one point of consciousness to another, from one side of the body to another, which gives rise to a new or alternative perceptual landscape. It is a moment of poetry. It can be a moment of vision.

> But to speak of Greek poetry is to speak of politics—not so much in the rarefied aesthetic sense of the old duality: poetry versus philosophy, that old Aristotelian kind of politics; rather, in the raw sense of poetry as crisis, as the rhythm and heartbeat of a nation's identity. And, politics as when a soldier says "in my *politike zoe* I am a carpenter," meaning in his "civilian life," using precisely the same term normally used for a "political life." Poetry, then, as one of the primary acts of the *zoon politikon*. And politics as when a civic model becomes workable *after* it has been heralded by the vanguard art of that culture, which has always been poetry. (Chioles 1993).

I have talked about history; now I can speak of the political. How is the political experienced on the level of the senses? The political and poetic have to be synthesized at the level of everyday experience. *Poesis* as a component of the everyday is crucial to the creation of the *zóon politikón*. This speaks to a politics of sensory creation and reception as a politics of everyday life.

More than that, *poesis* (poetry) means both making and imagining

(Seremetakis 1991). It thus takes various forms. Rehearing Diotima's response to Socrates,

> Any action which is the cause of something to emerge from nonexistence to existence is poesis, thus all craft works are kinds of poesis, and their creators are all poets. . . . Yet, they are not called, as you know, poets, but have different names; out of the general meaning of poetry, one part has been separated, that which deals with music and meter, and is given the name of the whole. Indeed this part alone is named poetry . . . (Plato 1976:150).

I can think of women's embroidering and weaving throughout the centuries. It always occured after daily routine labor. And although it involved work and the creation of articles of economic and symbolic value, it has always been experienced by women as a "resting moment." After ordering her immediate world, her household, the fields, she will halt, step back and begin to weave dreams, desires, musings into cloth. Women never embroider one piece or one design. They embroider series and sequences that cohere into a visual, tactile story. An embroidery piece captures a dream or an imaging, and women do not dream once. Such multiple, sequential production is not necessarily motivated by the accumulation of wealth or caused by economic circumstances demanding overproduction. It is their form of writing which, spread on cloths, ornaments and names people and spaces, within and beyond the household. Just like the ornaments Yannis Ritsos, the celebrated poet, left us: "To you I leave my clothes, my poems, my shoes. Wear them on Sundays." (Ritsos 1990).

The embroiderer, alone or with other women, borrows and elaborates the designs of others in a form of exchange. She is externalizing pieces of the self to make it public. Women circulate knowledge through multiple designs and spaces which they cover, protect and ornament. It is this transfer of the self into substance that disseminates a history of the person in dispersal. Embroidering engages a self-reflexive femininity: she will endow artifacts with her content and yet allow them to speak for themselves.

*   *   *

In one of my return trips to Greece, during our mid-day coffee, my mother opened a box she had been storing in her closet for years. One by one she took out dozens of beautiful embroidered and finely crocheted pieces of all shapes and sizes, made to ornament different parts of a house. As she displayed them she named each one after its maker, "This is from Voula for your name day last year," "This is from your aunt's friend two years ago for your book (publication)" and so on. As she spread them out I was taken through a journey to different times. A moment of stillness. These hand-made, tactile traces on the invisible past of my life represented their way of rendering me present in my absence. It was an imaginary historicization of my life-path and events which were inaccessible to those women as direct experience. Some of those donors I had never met, and others I knew very little; some I will not see again for they are long dead. Yet they, through narrative, knew me well. Well enough to exchange with my memory, as they embodied it in cloth. These gifts did not require a return—*"haláli sou,"* as they said.

* * *

I left Athens and traveled to the Peloponnese for my usual fieldwork. After I settled in my "first post," I looked out the window one morning and I had that irresistible desire to eat *hórta* (wild greens). I took a knife to collect them and jumped outside. Absorbed by the action, I heard the voice of a middle aged neighbor remarking on it, in the usual Greek way of asking a rhetorical question to state his approval: "Ah! your mother has taught you, eh?" Without thinking, and as he walked by, I smiled and nodded "yes." A few moments later I wondered "why on earth did I say yes?" Neither my mother nor anybody else as a matter of fact had taught me how to identify, select, cut and clean these greens. Suspicious of my harvest, I ran to a next door neighbor to check if it were edible. Although I had missed a few kinds, the ones I had collected were right. She also named them, thus I matched for the first time names I knew with the corresponding greens. Yet the question stuck in my mind: how did I know how to collect *hórta*? And more important, why didn't I have this skill and knowledge, nor the urge, to harvest *hórta* before I left Greece?

I had been eating *hórta* (boiled greens with oil, lemon and oregano) all my life, whether in Greece or Astoria, USA (though in Astoria, one finds only domestic substitutes). I had tasted them that is, and I had heard all kinds of talks around them. When I went out to collect them, the sensory memory of taste, order, orality stored in the body was transferred to vision and tactility. My body involuntarily knew what I consciously did not.

This knowing emerged in "exile." The absence of *hórta* and the memory of it shifted to the senses and to action. What was an outward act of cutting was in fact an inward act of diving into the self, of space-time and sensory compression, as well as of sensory switching that culminated in the harvesting. This was a resting point, a moment of stillness, where an entire past sensory landscape was translated into a present act; and in the course of doing so, one sense educated and encultured the other. This was an involuntary process, a moment of sensory stasis where one sense became the meta-narrative of another through memory. Thus sensory stasis is not always cultivated as in the mid-day coffee sipping. It can occur through forced experiences of crisis, separation and cross cultural contact. For these moments release hidden substances of the past. It is the very absence of referents, surfaces and textures that lifts them out of the banality of structural silence imposed by a culture or social order and allows a previously by-passed content to be released as history.

Notes

1. To conduct an etymological analysis of a term or concept is not to assume that all the sediments of meaning are operant at all times and with a uniform prevalence. However, etymological analysis is complementary to the uneven historical development of European peripheries which is characterized by the incomplete and disjunctive articulation of the pre-modern, different phases within modernity, and the post-modern. Etymology captures the uneven shifts of semantic history that may be present at any given moment in a society. Thus the American sense of the term nostalgia can be discerned in Greek state discourses and in the popular press. Both institutions tend to deliver discourses on identity and value loss and consequent societal crises. Yet, in its various etymological senses discussed here, *nostalghia* is widely heard in the language of everyday life, as well as in Greek popular music and poetry.

2. See my discussion and critique, in the Greek context, of rhetorical-display models of performance in *The Last Word* (1991).

3. The notions of authenticity and inauthenticity are symbiotic concepts that equally repress and silence non-contemporaneous and discordant cultural experiences and sensibilities. Thus the modernist critic would look at Greek society and dismiss any residues and incongruities emanating from the pre-modern as both romantic and invented (see for instance Hobsbawn and Ranger on Scotland (1985) and in the context of Greece, Faubion (1988). In both cases, static impositions of the polarity authentic/inauthentic led to the dismissal of important discontinuous cultural systems and sensibilities that have been repositioned within the modern as non-synchronous elements.

References

Benjamin, Walter. 1969. "The Work of Art in the Age of Mechanical Reproduction." *Illuminations*. Hannah Arendt, editor. Trans. H. Zohn. New York: Schocken, pp. 83–109, 217–51, 253–64.

———. 1973. *Charles Baudelaire: A Lyric Poet in the Era of High Capitalism*. Trans. Harry Zohn. London: NLB.

———. 1978. "Surrealism: The Last Snapshot of the European Intelligentsia." *Reflections*. New York: Harcourt Brace Jovanovich, pp. 177–92.

Bloch, Ernst. 1991. *Heritage of Our Times*. Trans. Neville & Stephen Plaice. Berkeley: University of California Press.

Chioles, John. 1993. "Poetry and Politics: The Greek Cultural Dilemma." *Ritual, Power and the Body: Historical Perspectives on the Representation of Greek Women.* C. Nadia Seremetakis, editor. New York: Pella Publishing Co. (Greek Studies), pp. 151–73.

Crary, Jonathan. 1991. *Techniques of the Observer: On Vision and Modernity in the Nineteenth Century.* Cambridge, Mass: MIT Press.

Douglas, Mary, ed. 1991. *Constructive Drinking: Perspectives on Drink from Anthropology.* Cambridge: Cambridge University Press.

Faubion, James. 1988. "Possible Modernities." *Cultural Anthropology,* vol.3 , no. 4, pp. 365–378.

Harvey, David. 1989. *The Condition of Postmodernity: An Inquiry into the Origins of Cultural Change.* Oxford: Blackwell.

Hobsbawm, Eric and Terence Ranger, editors. 1985. *The Invention of Tradition.* Cambridge: Cambridge University Press.

Jameson, Fredric. 1981. *The Political Unconscious: Narrative as a Socially Symbolic Act.* Ithaca: Cornell University Press.

Plato. 1976. (The Symposium) *Platonos Symposion.* I. Sikoutris, editor. Athens: Estia.

Ricoeur, Paul. 1984. *Time and Narrative.* Vol. 1. Chicago: University of Chicago Press.

Ritsos, Yannis. 1991. *3x111 Tristichs.* Trans. Rick Newton. New York: Pella Publishing Co. (Greek Studies).

Seremetakis, C. Nadia. 1984. "The Eye of the Other: Watching Death in Rural Greece." *Journal of Modern Hellenism,* vol. 1, no. 1, pp. 63–77.

———. 1991. *The Last Word: Women, Death and Divination in Inner Mani.* Chicago: University of Chicago Press.

———. 1993. "Gender, Culture and History: On the Anthropologies of Ancient and Modern Greece." *Ritual, Power and the Body: Historical Perspectives on the Representation of Greek Women.* C. Nadia Seremetakis, editor. New York: Pella Publishing Co. (Greek Studies).

———. 1994a. "Two Years After: The Last Word in Greece and Beyond." *The Last Word in the Ends of Europe: Divination, Death, Women.* C. Nadia Seremetakis. In Greek. Athens: Nea Synora/Livanis Publishing Co.

———. 1994b. "Gender Studies or Women's Studies: Theoretical and Paedagogical Issues, Research Agendas and Directions." (Keynote speech, UNESCO International Conference on Gender Studies, Athens 1993.) *Australian Feminist Studies,* Summer 1994.

2

Intersection:
Benjamin, Bloch, Braudel, Beyond

C. Nadia Seremetakis

The structure of modern sensory experience is inherently ironic. The sensory sphere is experienced in such a manner that profound transformations occurring in it or imposed on it are rendered imperceptible to the individual eye. This is precisely why everyday life in modernity has become the site for far-reaching historical transformations. For it is there that the historical unconscious is most powerful. Everyday life is experienced as a seamless continuum, an ongoing flow of ahistorical time, i.e., largely unnarrated temporality that surpasses individual and collective consciousness and language. This sensory structure of everyday life is experienced as naturalized, almost cosmic time over and against which eruptive, "sensational events" such as elections, performances, accidents, disasters, are profiled. The latter are almost pre-selected as narrated history, and certainly there is an ensemble of cultural, economic and political institutions and technologies devoted to their ongoing recitation. But the narrativity of the sensational event is itself made possible by a relation of foreground and background.

The polarity between the sensational and the mundane is also the dichotomy between the sensational and the sensory in which the latter is left unmarked, unvoiced and unattended to, as a banal element of the everyday. This division distinguishes the anonymous flow of the everyday from that which is culturally, politically and biographically set aside as notable and discursive. This cultural construction of the "public" and the sayable in turn creates zones of privatized, inadmissible memory and experience that operate as spaces of social amnesia and anaesthesia. Yet, what is experienced as a background of organic, continuous time is in fact a political-cultural creation. As the zones of amnesia and the unsaid expand in tandem with the increasingly formulaic and selective reproduction of public memory, the issue of narrativity becomes a zone of increasing political and cultural tension.

The split between public and private memory, the narrated and unnarrated, inadvertently reveals the extent to which everyday experience is
organized around the reproduction of inattention, and therefore the extent to which a good deal of historical experience is relegated to forgetfulness. The senses as the bearers and record-keepers of involuntary and
pervasive material experience, and therefore as potential sources of alternative memory and temporality are precisely that which is frequently
subjected to social forgetfulness and thereby constitute the sphere of hidden historical otherness.

The polarity between memory and inattention within historical consciousness roughly corresponds to two contrasting perspectives on
everyday life, that of Braudel (1976, 1980) and that of Benjamin (1969;
Buck-Morss 1989) and Bloch (1991). Braudel popularized the notion of
the *longue durée* which functions in his histories almost as a historical unconscious. The *longue durée* is constituted by the protracted economic,
ecological, biological processes and anonymous social practices of daily
life that elude intentionality and conscious experience and which invisibly deliver social orders to unavoidable historical junctures and consequences. The *longue durée* is both an analytic tool and an empirical description of historical experience in everyday life. As such it is also a
passageway into the social unconscious and the historical structure of
inattention. The *longue durée* may have been Braudel's symptomatic
response, at the level of theory, to the anonymity, immensity and complexity of everyday experience in modernity which certainly eluded the
historian's consciousness in a way that premodern "mentalities" did not.

Because Braudel did not explicity explore the social structure of inattention in his own epoch, his formulations tend to naturalize the historical unconscious, in its particular form as the *longue durée*, as an ahistorical and universal effect. The *longue durée* permeates all historical
experience with an amorphous determinism that hinders any account of
how it is replicated in time and space, particularly at the levels of personal practice and experience and socially constructed inattention. This
would entail an analysis of the intersection of consciousness and unconscious, of intentionality, act and consequence, of attention and inattention, and of the senses as "mentalities" in contrast to treating culture
solely as a passive effect of deeper and inaccessible historical constellations.

Benjamin and Bloch, twenty years prior to Braudel, posed the perceptual structure of everyday life in modernity as the experience of a claus-
trophobic cyclical and mythic continuum. This ideological continuum
was culturally and subjectively experienced in a manner similar to Braudel's *longue durée*. Modernity portrays and constructs itself as a self originating continuum selectively appropriating the past, and creating inat-

tention, in order to mandate the present and the future through the idea of progress—the meta-narrative of continuous and directional historical time. Within the continuum, normative and distilling perceptual grids are disseminated, which exclude whole spheres of historically discordant experience in favor of a dominant public memory of continuity and linearity. Both Benjamin and Bloch emphasized that the most efficacious and pernicious dimension of the constructed continuum was its appearance or presentation as natural. It was in this manner that the radical displacements of commodification and technology were normalized in everyday experience. Both theorists remarked on how new technologies and commodities were presented in the garb of archaic, customary and typified imagery and associations which supressed their disorienting cultural impact and foreclosed alternative social relations with these novelties. Another irony of modernity is its repetitiousness and monosemy to the extent that it valorized and re-enacted the continuous production of the new. These orientations were bound to have had an enormous impact on the perceptual structure of historical experience.

The unconscious experience of continuum in everyday life, which Braudel inadvertently presented as a given and almost "organic" dimension of historical experience, Benjamin and Bloch described as political-cultural construct; a myth by which the political order, in its widest term, is mediated and natured at the level of everyday perceptual experience and discourse. For Benjamin and Bloch, it was the continuum, as mythic premise, narration and iconography, that politically and culturally permeated every dimension of mundane social experience and which generated historical forgetfulness.

Both Benjamin and Bloch looked to discordant objects, experiences of discontinuity, and cultural zones of non-contemporaneity in everyday social practice as containing interruptive possibilities in relation to the dominant myth of the continuum. However, they both treated these counterpoints in an opportunistic theoretical fashion. It was largely a matter for the theorist to thematize and thus liberate the counter-codes and alternative perceptual experiences from everyday life. Thus they tended to ignore or undervalue the extent to which particular cultures and social strata had developed their own indigenous, self-reflexive practices which cultivated break, rupture, discontinuity and alterity in everyday modern life. Their relative blindness to this, may be attributed to the fact that their analyses was almost exclusively centered on Western European metropolitan cultures and in many ways addressed to the historical problem that the most vociferous resistance to modernity at that time was embodied by fascism.

Although they rejected all evolutionary theories as historical distortion, and as expressions of the ideology of the historical continuum, they rarely turned to those cultures and societies inside and outside of Europe that had undergone a historically uneven and incomplete articulation with the economic and ideological forms of European progress. It is precisely at these sites that we can locate staggered and discontinuous material cultures and landscapes, and popular narrative forms that issue diverse temporal and perceptual consciousnesses.

This is why I have turned to Greek cultural practices, etymologies and sensory orientations as examples of alternative perceptual epistemologies that have theoretical ramifications for general anthropology and beyond.

References

Benjamin, Walter. 1969. *Illuminations.* Ed. Hannah Arendt. Trans. H. Zohn. New York: Schocken, pp. 253–64.

Bloch, Ernst. 1991. *Heritage of Our Times.* Trans. Neville & Stephen Plaice. Berkeley: University of California Press.

Braudel, Fernand. 1980. *On History.* Trans. Sarah Matthews. Chicago: University of Chicago Press.

———. 1976. *The Mediterranean and the Mediterranean World in the Age of Philip II.* Vols. 1 & 2. New York: Harper & Row.

Buck-Morss, Susan. 1989. *The Dialectics of Seeing: Walter Benjamin and the Arcades Project.* Cambridge, Mass: MIT Press.

3

The Memory of the Senses, Part II: Still Acts

C. Nadia Seremetakis

This is an essay in six acts—Prelude, Saliva, the Journey, Traffic, Dust, and Reflexive Commensality—that explore the senses and material culture as exchange, memories, ethnographic description, and as a conceptual problematic of fieldwork and modernity. The montage of these impinging fragments concurs with my proposal that the numbing and erasure of sensory realities are crucial moments in socio-cultural transformation. These moments can only be glimpsed at obliquely and at the margins, for their visibility requires an immersion into interrupted sensory memory and displaced emotions. Thus the use of montage here is not simply an aesthetic or arbitrary choice. Sensory and experiential fragmentation is the form in which this sensory history has been stored and this dictates the form of its reconstruction. For I believe that there can be no reflexivity unless one passes through a historical reenactment of perceptual difference.

Montage also reflects the transactional dimensions of my research in rural and urban Greece on sensory experience, memory and material history which combines traditional fieldwork inquiry with the biographical experience of my generation; a generation that straddles the admixture of rural and urban economies and cultures that has taken place since the post war period. In fusing the ethnographic and the biographical I focus on everyday language use, and the symbolic and affective dimensions of material culture as passageways into those experiential fragments, deferred emotions and lost objects that were not part of the public culture of Greek modernization, yet were integral to the tangible force of its historical passage. The mixture of fieldwork inquiry, biography and narrative styles here also refracts the ready-made montage that organizes that hybrid figure called the "native anthropologist"; a figure that is the very embodiment of the syncretism of incomplete modernization.

Prelude

Grandma used to mash with her fingers carrot, potato, macaroni, and feel it with her lips and even her tongue and then give it to the child. Although the food was not always hot, this movement from hands to lips was repeated automatically. This was not only done by grandmas but also by any older woman of the neighborhood who was like a relative to the family.

When she finished feeding the child, she would kiss its "dirty" mouth [*leroméno stomatáki*], she would "dance" it up and down, calling it "my pride," "my heart," "my little moon," "my roses [referring to its lips]," "my seashells [*kohilákia*, referring to the ears]," and other sweet names. But sometimes also "big head" [*kefála*],when the head was large or the child stubborn. Such nick-names haunted you for the rest of your life. I was for instance called *tsaknarídha* because my legs were too skinny like *tsákna*, little twigs. There was no part of the body that they did not have something good or bad to say about, giving it a good or bad name. For example, thick uncombed, unruly hair would be named *afána*, the wild bush. And then you, as a whole, were called *afána*.

When the food was hard, such as bread crust, the old women would soften it with their saliva. Also, when we ran back home with a wound of some sort, they put saliva on it with their finger to heal it. When we were crying, they took saliva from their mouth and with their fingers wiped the corners of our eyes and cheeks. If we had smudges [*moutzoúres*] on the face or hands, they often "washed" us with their saliva. All women used saliva for cleaning and healing and one time my father too.

When they had the baby in their arms, dancing it, they would give it the characteristics of the grandpa or the grandma. If the grandpa had a moustache for instance, although the baby had none, they would say, as if already seeing it, "he will become a great moustache when he grows up." If the grandpa was a good dancer they would relate the baby's dangling legs to dancing. Or if he was a musician or simply liked music, they were capable of seeing the baby with a violin in its hands.

And what of fairy tales? When we were in the country [referring to a small town in Central Greece], grandma gathered us by the fireplace and the kerosene lamp. And she began, "*Kókini klostí dheméni stin anémi tiligméni dhóstou klótso na ghirísi paramythi narhinísi. Mía forá ki éna keró*" [Red thread tied to the spindle and wrapped around, give it a kick to turn for the fairy tale to begin. Once upon a time . . .] She spoke of fairies [*neráidhes*], princesses, but also animals such as the female piggy [*ghourounítsa*] called Rinoúla, who stole food from wedding-feasts making a mess and leaving people wondering who had done these things. And the hen who had magical qualities like all animals in grandma's fairy tales. The hen could suck up an entire river with her ass. *"Roúfa kóle to potámi"* [Ass! Suck up the river!] the hen would command in order to cross it, or to allow the hero to cross. Or if there was fire she put it out by letting the river out. Women would often turn their own past life into fairy tales to tell the kids. The kids loved to hear who mistreated them, or loved them in their families, clan, neighborhood in their childhood. Grandma would stand up and play the heroes like the hen and the piggy. I believe fairy tales like Rinoula the piggy were created by her on the spot. Also real stories, news spreading through the neighborhood, were retold to children as fairy tales and presented as stories from the old days. After we grew up, we often learned that these had been recent happenings.

When children died they told us they were up in the sky, and the stars of the sky [*asterákia touranoú*] were their eyes or the little candles they held to light up the earth.

In the morning the gypsy would pass with his *défi* [hand drum]. We were running out to see his monkey putting on lipstick, shaking hands, pretending the lady.

Once a man fell in love with a young woman, Lenió, who died, so he went crazy. He was the madman who roamed the neighborhood. We imitated his strange talk in the house. At times a group of us took a big stone, ornamented it with flowers, took it to him and told him this was Lenió. He would take it in his hands, talk to it, cry and mourn as if it were Lenió. We were weeping too. There was a moment I remember that I, at least, believed the stone was Lenió. Afterwards we couldn't just throw it out. We took her carefully with him together and buried her in a ditch.

Then the *akonistís* who sharpened the knives would appear in the neighborhood, then the *lanarás* who treated the wool, the *yirológos* who brought all kinds of little things for sale, the *salepitzís*, who sold a thick drink from Turkey, the women with loads of woods on their backs to sell, the *xilopódharos* who walked on high stilts with all the children of neighborhood following him, the man with the *latérna* [hurdy-gurdy], the street photographer, the fishmonger carrying on his head a flat wicker tray full of fish, resting on a towel twisted around his head. And various vendors selling chestnuts, oregano and sage brought from afar, old lady's hair [cotton candy] and many other things. In the summer nights, when we played in the streets very late, we would also see the drunkard. I remember all these in the 40's and 50's, after the war, in Athens.

—*Elpida's recollections,
Summer 1991, Athens*

Saliva

The grandma dressed in black, sitting at home or at the edge of the fields, feeds the baby.[1] The baby in the cradle or on her lap is wrapped tightly in strips of cloth. She takes a piece of crustless bread, the inside of the bread known as *psíha*, crumbles it with her fingers and puts a few crumbs in her toothless mouth. The tongue, rotating, moistens the bread with saliva till it becomes a paste, "clay." She molds the bread till its texture signals that it is ready for the child. She takes the bread from her mouth and places it in its toothless mouth.[2] The baby swallows it as she swallows her saliva flavored by the bread. Her fingers reach for more bread and the act is repeated. On other occasions she dips the crumbs first in olive oil before molding them with her saliva. She talks and chants to the baby, calling to it: "my eyes," "my heart," "my soul," "my bread loafs" (*frajolítses mou*—when referring to the pudgy white legs), "my crown." She continues till the baby sleeps, both waiting for its mother to return from the fields.[3]

Different names pertain to this process of feeding a child in various parts of Greece. In the Southern Peloponnese, for instance, this child has been "raised" with *masoulíthres* or *ladhopsíhala* (the former derives from the verb *masáo*, to chew; the latter from the nouns *ládhi*, olive oil, and *psíhala*, bread crumbs). They are described as clay-like substance (*pilós*) resembling that prepared by the birds to feed their little ones in the nest. The process of raising a child is known as "resurrecting a child" (*anasténo pedhí*). This child will often be described as having been "resurrected with *masoulíthres* by his grandma" (*anastíthike me masoulíthres* or *i yiayiá tou to anástise*). The notion of resurrection is connected to the movement from down to up, from death to life, from sleeping to awakening, and from the raw to the baked (cooked). A woman raises a child as she raises dough into bread. Working the bread with the tongue and the saliva, the grandma changes it to dough which is then used to raise the child. Raising here is akin to baking. Children are also "baked in the ocean." There the "salt and sun bake the child" (*to psínoun*) transforming a pale body into a "crusty skin." Baking gives form: color, shape, texture. Enculturation is a sensory process and tied to the acquiring of form. It draws its imagery (color, shape, texture) from the body and food processing. There is no rigid dichotomy between enculturating and natural processes that transform the body. Northerners, for instance, or dull persons are often characterized as "raw" or "dough" or "inedible" precisely because they are not properly enculturated (raised) in Greek ways. Baking results in an upward movement: coffee is "baked" until it rises to form a top (*kaimáki*)—the top implies sedimentation, texture in taste. Bread and deserts are baked to rise and/or till they form a crust. When they are not raised, they are not "ready" and thus considered "raw"; as Greeks say, "pale like dead." The stiff, raw and dead can be raised to life, can be baked. The raw food is termed *omó*—which is also a metaphor for the uncultivated person.

Baking involves the alternation between raising (the up) and sleeping (the down). The act of baking and cooking, in general, is always a trial. The cook "has to be fully alert" because cooking is a sudden awakening of substance and the senses. It is often said after a dish has finished cooking, "Let it sleep now, let it rest." The cook also rests at this point; most of the time she does not eat the food she prepares for others, for she is "filled with the smells."

The child is resurrected because the passage from the womb is a passage out of the dark and from a state of sleep. Babies are wrapped in cloth, and the dough is covered with blankets and towels to rise. The mouth of the grandma (softening the bread) is an oven, as is the womb (see also duBois 1988). The grandma feeding the baby with her mouth is resurrecting it by awakening its body point by point, by calling and naming points[4] (*semía*) of the body: "my eyes," "my heart," "my soul," or "my olive"[5] referring to a birth mark. These are inferential codes for a complex act that engages other parts and points of the body not explicitly named. The entire act of feeding the child and naming the points of the body is an awakening of the senses. The act of talking to the child engages hearing. Naming the eyes awakens vision, the transference of substance from mouth to mouth animates taste and tactility.

The act of calling and naming is also an act of exchange. The substance transferred from the mouth of the grandma to the mouth of the child is her saliva, her taste or flavor, that becomes its own taste. It is food baked within her, with parts of her, her substance which is then transferred. This act can be contrasted to the feeding of the child with baby food from a jar bought in the store. By naming the child's gaze "my eyes," the grandma exchanges body parts and establishes vision as a social and sensory reciprocity. She calls the child "my heart" for the emotions in this awakening are as sensual as the senses are emotive. This act of sharing and naming parts and senses constructs one heart for two bodies, as one food was baked with saliva for two mouths, as one soul is raised for two persons, as one pair of eyes is imprinted on two bodies. The grandma gives her parts to see them inscribed on the child over time. *This is what she receives back from the child: the memory of herself in parts.*

The points of the body once awakened are not merely marks on the surface but are an active capacity. Awakening these points as sensate is opening the body to semiosis. The senses, the "points" (*semía*) of the body, are the sites where matter is subjected to signification. Semiosis here is inseparable from interpersonal exchange. The child is not only exposed to substance but to *shared substance*. The grandma's molding of the bread crumbs with saliva is a transcription of the self onto matter which is then transferred into the body of the child. This is the materialization of the person and the personification of matter.[6] The transcription of self onto substance and then into the child's body is inseparable from the transmission of emotions as a fuel of this exchange—which is why this is understood as "one heart for two bodies." Or as the sayings go, "we are one breath," "we are one home," we grew up "with one food, one water."

The act of exchange is registered on the senses that seal it as a social relation. In turn, the senses are synchronized and crossed with each other and with *the Other*, so that senses and subjects can witness and be witnessed. "Listen to see" is the colloquial Greek phrase to demand attention in conversation; or "I can(not) hear it"[7] in reference to tasting a food flavor. The memory of one sense is stored in another: that of tactility in sound, of hearing in taste, of sight in sound. Sensory memory is a form of storage. Storage is always the embodiment and conservation of experiences, persons and matter in vessels of alterity. The awakening of the senses is awakening the capacity for memory, of tangible memory; to be awake is to remember, and one remembers through the senses, via substance. Cooking food in grandma's mouth with saliva imprints memory on the substance internalized by the child. Memory is stored in substances that are shared, just as substances are stored in social memory which is sensory.

Grandma feeding the child is also resurrecting it from death as a kind of generational sleep. She feeds the child that is often named after herself, her husband or one of her dead children. Personal names are passed down in families through alternate generations. This naming system endows the exchange of food, body parts and senses with a historical sensibility—which is why it is all the more important for the senses and memory to witness and to record (historicize) the acts of exchange.[8] In this context, the food is not only cooked by saliva but also by emotions and memory. In turn, social memory is baked (raised) and thus reproduced by awakening the child. The dead can be raised through cooking, eating, awakening and exchanging, which all require memory. Ceremonial eating follows all death rituals.

The storage of memory in the senses, which awakens both, is based, like any other form of storage, on deferred consumption. Women in this culture distribute before they consume. Cooking is always for others. Cooking defers the immediacy of consumption. This is epitomized by the grandma who molds the food in her mouth and instead of swallowing it, places it in the mouth of the baby. A common Greek expression is "she was taking the food out of her mouth to feed him" referring literally to how one was raised and metaphorically to how two people relate; another expression of exchange is "you eat and I am filled." The deferment of consumption is affective because one always cooks for significant others. To defer and to store is to place into alterity, the self registering substance and emotions in the other. Storage by both donor and recipient encodes the material world. If matter was to be subjected to immediate consumption, there would be no senses, no semiosis, and no memory. The senses defer the material world by changing substance into memory.

The return to the senses (experiential or theoretical), therefore, can never be a return to realism; to the thing-in-itself, or to the literal. In realism, matter is never deferred, but supposedly subjected to total consumption. When the child returns to the senses, this passage will always be mediated by memory, and memory is concerned with, and assembled from, sensory and experiential fragments. This assemblage will always be an act of imagination—thus opposed to the reductions of realism.[9]

The Journey

The child, now living in the city, returns to visit the grandma in the country. The trip to the village to visit grandma was by train. It meant camping out on a long journey. This entailed elaborate preparations, such as the packing of functional items for surviving the trip and numerous gifts for friends and relatives. Every station was identified with specific foods, their particular tastes and smells—one station with *souvláki*, another with rice pudding, pistachios, *pastéli*, dried figs. The child traveled through substances to reach grandma; a journey that sharpened the senses and prepared the child for diving into the village. The child arrived to the smell of the ocean, the trees—lemon, orange, olive—the sound of the donkey's bray, and the omnipresent, loud, loud music of the cicadas: sensory gates that signified entry into a separate space. The child greets the grandma who has been surveying the road like a gatepost, and passes into her world through the smells and texture of her dress. Shoes are removed as the child enters the main door and the pebbled floor leaves an indelible mark on the insteps. Its feet soon move from the hard pebbled floor to the soft mud of the gardens soothing its insole; an ingestion of the wet and the dry through the insole. Tactility extends beyond the hands.

There is also a tactility of smells. Each smell generates its own textures and surfaces. No smell is encountered alone. There are combinations of smells that make up a unified presence, the grandma's house: the garden aroma combined with the animal dung; the oreganon bunch hanging over the sheep skin containing the year's cheese; the blankets stored in the cabinet which combine rough wool with the humidity of the ocean; the oven exuding the smell of baking bread and the residue of the ashes;

the fresh bread in the open covered with white cotton towels. Nothing is sealed for the sake of preserving. To do so would mean to silence the smells preventing them from being "heard." As one moves from place to place in the house and gardens, these smells come in waves.

The senses in this place are moving constantly, they are not stationary. They blend, combine and recombine, shifting positions and transforming contexts. The fig is on the tree in the field one day, and next morning hundreds of figs are gathered and placed on bamboo mats on the beach, by the ocean to sundry. They look like pebbles and their strong sour taste blends with the smell of the sea. Then comes the olive season or the noodle making. For smells have seasons and each season smells. There is no watermelon in the winter, for instance, as in America. For taste has seasons too, and each season tastes. Each season also has its colors, as well as its sounds: cicadas, winds, ocean, earth.

Traffic

The grandma sits on a wooden stool, her legs comfortably spread apart with her skirt around them forming an armchair. Her face dark, her hair tied in a bun, her hands freckled and rough. The child slips into her lap. It is time for fairy tales. Slipping into her lap is slipping into a surround of different smells and textures, sediments of her work in the fields, the kitchen, with the animals. Through the anxieties of the parents, the child has learned that the grandma is the person who places it in contact with things dangerous and improper. She is the one who has a different relation to water, its qualities and economy, and thus to washing. She is the one who introduces "dirt."

She cracks a walnut. She "cleans" the inside, the "bread" (psíha), by peeling off the thin membrane that covers it. She splits the inside into pieces and reveals the parts of a new cosmos. She is a woman in the middle of chickens, dogs, cats, rabbits, goats, wells, mountains, oceans. These become the material emblems of her fairy tales, and the countryside the allegory of her stories. The landscape exhibits the fragments and ruins of her tales; its topography becomes a narrative sequence in itself. Her stories, inscribing the ocean, will come in waves. Yet, these tales are not the mere combination of her physical world. Outside invisible forces crack the surface and pop up to disorder and repatch that reality. Pirates and brigands raiding the ocean, monsters in the mountains, bad and good fairies fighting, snakes laying in ambush for passersby, ghosts talking, guiding and misguiding you. In one instance a child will be born by popping out from the woman's calf. The parts of the body, like the parts of the world, are mobilized; parts that were stationary and insignificant. These parts now recombined begin to signify. This is a repatching of the human body and of the "body" of the world.

This recombination and mobilization of the "body" through the fairy tale is staged on the grandma's own body in the way she performs and tells her story. Through breathing, vocal tones and gestures, her body enacts all the forces, characters and movements of the story. As the grandma and child eat the walnut, the fairy tale and its telling become the saliva on the "bread" of the present, bringing the past into the child's mouth.

Next morning the sea will no longer be the sea, a flat surface for play. It will also be a surface cracked by the raiding pirates. In this cosmos, the unexpected, the incongruous will appear suddenly from the casual and the everyday through their interruption and transformation. Sitting in between her legs, the child is split between two worlds like the tree in her fairy tales that grows in between two rocks which make its abode; a split home formed by a stereoscopic vision ignited by the fairy tales in which the past and the present, the phantasmagoric and the everyday are juxtaposed on the material landscape and the senses.

When the fairy tale is remembered through play in the city, the child's new stereoscopic vision infiltrates the urban space, the city apartment, the parlor and the bedroom, creating an alternative geography. Within the apartment, the child will uncover obscure spaces, corners, closets that will become separate and imaginary and within which the fairy tales will be reenacted. These can be "old rooms" or unfinished rooms and alcoves which contain discarded objects of all sorts, colors and shapes. They become artifacts, actors of the fairy tale landscape. On the street old buildings, abandoned buildings, or buildings under construction will be transformed into "open" spaces for the transcription of the fairy tale surround.

Through her fairy tale (*paramythi*), the grandma brings the past into the present as a transformative and interruptive force. This very action defines the efficacy of the fairy tale as post-mythic—something related to myth but beyond it, a narrative that extracts and liberates, disassembles and reassembles the substance and fragments of myth in order to create passageways between times and spaces. Just as she chops up the landscape of the countryside rearranging its parts in order to convey her tales, the infiltration of the child's present by these narratives chops into pieces its world picture, undermining surface coherence with foreign elements. The fairy tale as narrative, performance and persona is post-mythic to the extent that it challenges and decenters contemporary myths that divorce and segregate the past from the present; myths that respectively depict the past and the present as separate homogeneities. The grandma's narration hooks things, shifting them from one space and time to another. This narrative redistribution interrupts the present as a closed continuum because it inserts and works with objects and experiences that are qualified by their spatial and temporal strangeness. Thus she becomes a colporteur[10] similar to the journeyman, the carnival performer, the sailor, who are comfortable moving between the city and the country and who bring with them glittering trinkets and other exotica; everyday objects from different sites and epochs. Colporteurs tell stories of the exotic and the different with artifacts as well as with language. Their stories, their small goods are bits and pieces of alterity that bring with them semantic possibility in miniature.

A characteristic figure of colportage, in urban and rural Greece has been the *pramateftís* or *yirológos* (*práma* means thing, event—deriving from the verb *pramatévo* which means I handle, trade, deal with, or put together; *yíro* means (a)round, and *lógos* discourse). Both terms concern the circulation of things, words, signs, and sounds, as nonseparable elements of trafficking, understood as a symbolic, performative and economic practice—a way of telling stories with objects and a way of circulating other cultures and their objects through stories. Colporteurs have also been repairmen of all sorts, fruit and vegetable vendors, fishmongers who traveled with donkeys and later motorcycle trucks, the newspaper man, and earlier the gypsy with his little monkey that danced to the tunes of the *défi* (a drum) and caricatured known personalities. On special days in the cities, this traffic was joined by the *ghaitanáki*, a carnival figure of a donkey formed by two men under a frame covered with multicolored strips of paper and dancing to the beat of a drum played by a third man. All these figures, along with the sailor and the returned emigrant, created a traffic of exotica, an alternative economy that transcended urban/rural spatial and temporal boundaries within a periphery. Many of them were also envoys of an invisible market network that connected this periphery with the markets of other peripheries in distant parts of the world, all of which bypassed and/or exploited dominant economies.

This traffic was a choreographed time-keeping mechanism. Hours, days, and seasons were measured in alternating performances, each accompanied by its sounds, smells, textures and visual spectacle. Colporteurs were figures stepping on and off the road as if it were a public stage, and in the eyes of the child they were akin to the fairy tale as the entry of the "fantastic" into the everyday.

There was traffic at night as well. When all movement stopped, the drunkard would appear. Staggering and stuttering, he passed next to low windows scaring everybody, especially the children. The drunkard of the urban neighborhoods, singing and grumbling against the world, interrupting the silence of the night was feared though tolerated. Nobody would call the police. He was the scarecrow people would play with but not expel.

The ingredients of colportage, the scattered contents of the unpacked

myth, that is disseminated through fairy tales and exotic traffic ornamented the everyday character of the child's present, lending it new
auras. Colportage has nothing to do with completed appearances and
geometric closures; rather in ornamenting the everyday with the sensibility of the different it cuts up the edifice of the routine and prosaic, it
forms fragments and animates broken up pieces of multiple realities in
transit. This is the migration of sensory forms via material artifacts, and
the memory they leave behind. The traffic of exotic matter here is both
literal and symbolic, actual and remembered; the transport (*metaphorá*) of
artifacts and narratives from one historical or cultural site to another is
their metaphorization. Therefore colportage and its engagement with
what can be shifted and altered is neither nostalgic nor realist.

In colportage, moments of the past and the different are glued onto the
experience of the present. This is both montage and the fermentation of
non-synchronicity in the present. Colportage is not the transfer of parts
and meanings into predetermined functions nor is it mechanical substitution.[11] With her saliva and stories, the grandma glues past generational
and collective history onto present biographical experience. This dynamic traces how the imaginary and mythic postures of one generation
are received within the childhood experience of another. The colportage
of the grandma and its witnessing by the child does not fashion a non-
contradictory totality. The grandma and child collaborate in the sensory
and narrative refiguration of the rural landscape; a refiguration that also
functions as a meta-commentary on the urban landscape because it
recharges the marginalized and the ephemeral within the urban with
exotic[12] meanings. This transcoding is all the more poignant because
within modernity and between the rural and the city landscapes, the
worlds of memory are rapidly replaced. Through the underground passageways between grandma and grandchild, through saliva and fairy
tale, through evocations of persons, dead and/or supernatural, and
through shared food, an alternative world of memory is set up against
the structure of repression and displacement called modernity.

*   *   *

Once upon a time my son
a good king ruled over a far away land

I remember to this day grandma starting
this way, her mind sailing in different times,
tenderly talking to me of this and that
witchcraft, love and great killings
Of good young kings who
conquered castles, killed the witches
and defeated monsters

And when the sweet sleep targeted my mind
my thought returned to the world of the fairy tales

Bad times took away from my dreams,
along with my joy, grandma's stories
They often come back from the old times
—God if it were only true—
like a gust of wind, those fairy tales

Don't cry my little girl for you open
wounds on my chest,
the two of us will make the world
a fairy tale.

—*Grandma's Fairy Tales, Cretan* mandinádha
composed and sung by the Cretan group
Hainidhes, popular among Greek youth

Dust

When the grandma comes from the village to visit her children in the
urban center, she has to be patched up to appear publicly in the metropole. This is a montaging that only the grandchild can read. For occasions like a family wedding or baptism, grandma is taken to the hair-
dresser to get her hair fixed, given a hat with a veil, a matching suit or
dress, special shoes that constrain her feet, a small purse otherwise useless to her, with some money and a handkerchief placed in it so it won't
be empty. She is dressed and staged in this manner to make an appearance for she is the hidden element of her children's past. In the city she is
the exposure of the inside to the outside, the rural to the urban. It is at
this moment that the grandchild catches the present fabricating the past.
The child is between two loving worlds and split into two, as if in between two mirrors never able to capture its full image in any one of them.

For the grandma this dressing up and ornamentation is inappropriate
to her life cycle where one only dresses this way for death. She can sense
that she is modernized as an element of a no longer pertinent reality
which is now named "the past." For the grandchild, however, the dressing of the grandma transforms her into a re-decorated artifact. The ex-
traction of the grandma from her rural context and her transformation
becomes in the child's perception analogous to its own coercive extrac-
tion from imaginary places and play and its insertion into an adult
world. Dressing up the grandma forms a dialectical image in which two
failed utopian expectations or sensibilities converge within the same
form: that of the rural and that of the urban. In this simultaneous investi-
ture and divestiture of the grandma, the child witnesses the repression of
the rural, its historical vulnerability and at the same time the inability of

modernity to fully transform the grandma. There is one such "grandma" in every other Greek household.

In comparison with the sensory layers and residues with which grandma is dressed in the village, she is now covered with "dead" objects. In this masquerade, she becomes the negated past, a fossilized display in the urban museum: the living room, the parlor. The deadening of the rural "past" and its framing in the parlor-museum transforms the sensory alterity of the grandma into dust. Dust is the perceptual waste material formed by the historical-cultural repression of sensory experience and memory. It is also the form that residual culture takes once it is compartmentalized as the archaic and sundered from any contemporary pertinence and presence.

Throughout the Mediterranean, the undusted house is a "dead" house, very much like the rural house "devoured" by overgrown weeds or abandoned by emigration (Seremetakis 1991). Dust offends the senses. It is the loss of the home to otherness: the temporal effacement of its semantic "surface," and its historical sedimentation. There is a relation between the accumulation of dust and the displacement of memory. The dust covered surface is alien to that sensory sedimentation that characterizes the grandma's house as a storage site of sensory memory where no odor or tactility is sealed—where not even the soil, the dirt with its smell and texture, can be left to become "dust," i.e., agriculturally dormant.

In Greek exhumation practices, women mourners, after bringing the bones up from below the earth and back into their perceptual field, dust, wash, and sun-dry the bones. This eliminates any foreign particle on the bone and restores the legibility of the artifact which is to be used as divination text. Without dusting they cannot "see" the bone in the divinatory sense nor touch it in the emotional sense. To make sensory contact with the bone without cleaning it, is to touch only the "dust." It is as if the bone, artifact of the remembered dead, has its own senses always in communication with the mourner's memory which can be blocked by the dust. Yet the dust is not devoid of signification. The dust on the bones and their cleaning encapsulates a material allegory of the temporal chasm that separates the living from the dead. This is the distance that is crossed by exhumation, an act of ritual purification that is understood as a sensory restoration and awakening of both the mourner and the bones which places them in communication. This awakening through the senses is divination (Seremetakis 1991).

In modernity dust forms around the culturally hollow space of the old that has been emptied of all indigenous meaning but which leaves its traces behind. Antiquarian, "tribal" and "folk" exotica inserted into the parlor space and then defined, encysted, encased and isolated as dust, emerge as fossilized displays, as a collector's artifact—a direct antithesis of the sensory mobility of living colportage. The past collected and encased is the past devoid of semantic possibilities because its meaning has been completed, exhausted, totalized and consumed; that is, turned to historical dust. Historical and cultural difference introduced into the parlor settles in as surface without depth, devoid of the record of exchanges that produced it; thus devoid of emotions, memory and the senses.

In the late 19th and early 20th centuries, the process of collecting, staging and displaying exotica, archaicized the past and domesticated cultural otherness. This interiorization was mediated by a circuit of spaces of containment, typified by the urban parlor, a space which communicated with the museum and the academic study. The logic of the museum was inscribed into the parlor, and the museum itself was inhabited and enjoyed as an enlarged public living room. The parlor/museum encapsulates western modernity's petrifaction and consumption of ethnological and historical difference. In parlor sites, items of older periods and other cultures which had their particular aromatic, tactile, and auditory realities were desensualized and permitted a purely visual existence. In this process, vision itself was desensualized and subsequently metaphorized as and reduced to a transparent double of the mind unmediated by any material, spatial and temporal interference (Corbin 1986; Foucault 1979; Fabian 1983). The taming of difference through sensory neutralization, fabricated a false historical continuity between past and present through the cover of dust. The history of fieldwork, the anthropology of the senses and the archaeology of dust are linked to the extent that spatial devices like the parlor and the museum mediated the modern perceptual experience of culture-bound sensory alterity. The encounter with the ethnographic other was filtered by the spatial containment and sensory repression of the parlor exhibit.

In the first decades of the 20th century, fieldwork and ethnography were informed by the impulse to exit from spaces of epistemological, textual and artifactual containment, such as the academic study and the ethnological museum—sites that were cultural variants of the parlor. Recent criticism emanating from within the discipline and from post-colonial sites inadvertently disclose the spatial and sensory continuity between parlor site and field site (see Fabian 1983; Asad 1975). Fieldwork depended on spatial instruments such as the political geography of colonial pacification and tribalization. These spatializing grids were reinforced by parlor-like sensory orientations and homogenizing representational strategies that privileged vision-centered consumption of ethnographic experience, the reductive mapping of cultural traits, and the narrative genre of a static ethnographic present (Clifford 1988; Fabian 1983). This flattening of cross-cultural sensory experience into visual diagrams and atemporal spatial metaphors exported the parlor to the field site and transformed the latter into an open air museum.

I shout to the dust
to disarm me.
I call the dust
by its code name: totality.

—from *"Unexpectancies"* by Kiki
Dimoula (trans. John Chioles)[13]

Reflexive Commensality

Between grandma and grandchild sensory acculturation and the materialization of historical consciousness occurred through the sharing of food, saliva and body parts. Another expression of this type of reciprocity is encountered in Maniat mourning ceremonies (Seremetakis 1990, 1991) where the lament circulates from mouth to mouth among singers as a shared substance. This sharing imparts a material density to the antiphonic exchanges of mourners from which oral history emerges. In Greek exhumation practices, the sensory presence of the dusted bones of the dead reawakens the memory of past commensal exchanges with the dead. Ignited by the collective memories invested in the bone as emotive artifact, the exhumers create a commensal ritual grounded on material substances, present and absent (past).

Commensality here *is not* just the social organization of food and drink consumption and the rules that enforce social institutions at the level of consumption. Nor can it be reduced to the food-related senses of taste and odor. *Commensality can be defined as the exchange of sensory memories and emotions, and of substances and objects incarnating remembrance and feeling.* Historical consciousness and other forms of social knowledge are created and then replicated in time and space through commensal ethics and exchange. Here each sense witnesses and records the commensal history of the others. In this type of exchange, history, knowledge, feeling and the senses become embedded in the material culture and its components: specific artifacts, places and performances. In processes of historical transformation and/or cross cultural encounter, divergent sensory structures and commensalities can come into conflict with each other, and some are socially repressed, erased or exiled into privatized recollection and marginal experience. These dynamics indicate profound transformations in a society's relation to material culture and to systems of knowledge bound up with the material.

The history of the senses in modernity (see Corbin 1986; Vigarello 1988; Gay 1984; Crary 1991) can be understood as the progressive effacement of commensality; that is, of a reflexive cultural institution that produced and reproduced social knowledge and collective memory through the circulation of material forms as templates of shared emotion and experience. In modernity, commensality is not absent but is rendered banal, functional or literal and increasingly reserved for the diversions of private life.[14] Yet commensality leads an underground existence as a repressed infrastructure of social knowledge (see also Marcus 1991).[15] In current ethnographic discourse commensality either has the status of fieldwork anecdote, or it is reified as a discrete object of inquiry internal to the culture of the Other. This is a curious pattern in a discipline that frequently worries over its own commodification of ethnographic knowledge, and which associates its progress with the recent expansion of surfaces of knowledge-consumption resulting from the multiplication of subdisciplines and specializations.

How can inquiry into the commensal practices of other cultures be undertaken when researchers do not consider nor generate accounts of the historical formation-repression of commensal ethics and sensory recipocities within their own culture and particular discipline?[16] Is there a commensal structure for the social production of knowledge in anthropology? Does this structure communicate with the organization of the senses and material culture in modernity? If so how does this affect the ethnographer's perception of the commensalities of cultural others?

*   *   *

The relation between dust and what it covers is not a relation of appearance and essence. It is a relation of historical sedimentation. *Dust is not deposited only on the object but also on the eye.* Sensory numbing constructs not only the perceived but also the perceiving subject and the media of perception; each of these are reflexive components of an historical process. Thus dust can be a subject of historical analysis just as much as the senses, objects and experiences that dust interrupts and blurs.

When the anthropologist first enters the field site, the sensory organization of modernity, the perceptual history and commensal structure of the discipline direct her/him to first see dust. Without long-term fieldwork and sensory archaeology the anthropologist may never come to know that this dust is a surface residue of the researcher's own acculturation that obscures depth: other sensory surfaces that embody alternative materialities, commensalities and histories. Without a reflexive anthropology of the senses, fieldwork, short[17] or long-term, remains trapped in the literal, captive of realist conventions that are themselves unacknowledged, historically determined perceptual and commensal patterns. This is well understood by those who inhabit the memory of other sensory and material reciprocities. How can they take anthropologists seriously if the latter go with the dust?

*　　*　　*

"When I die, I am going to leave this gold tooth for you." "But Grandmother, how are you going to pull it out once you are cold and gone?" . . .
"You'll pull it out."

Empty the table, and over the emptiness, dust. Over the dust the habitual searching of your bony fingers. Is it a candle, or a tooth? Whenever I see
that glow in the dark I'll know it's you coming home to visit. (Excerpt from
Stratis Haviaras's novel, *When the Tree Sings*)

Notes

1. Given the incomplete and uneven character of capitalist penetration and
modernization in Greece and the accelerated rural to urban migration, which still
allows for reverse seasonal migration (back to the country), the structure of the
Greek family particularly from the perspective of a generational profile, can span
rural and urban economies and cultures (for a fuller discussion, see Seremetakis
1991). Therefore in Greece as in other cultures that have undergone similar uneven transformations, e.g., Latin America, the grandmother has been a central
and ubiquitous figure in the popular imagination, literature and cinema representing the anomalous persistence of the past in a present that has not superseded
it.

2. Mutual toothlessness points to the twinship of grandma and child as limi-
nal figures in this social context. Greek folk-sayings and humor on the mimetic
relations between old age and infancy are common; they concern the lack of teeth
and the inability to consume "adult," that is, hard food. The elderly frequently
comment with irony on this resemblance. For instance, the perceived similarity
between the physical, mental and social aspects of the life-cycle stages of old-age
and infancy, informs the organization and intensity of mourning rituals in Inner
Mani (see Seremetakis 1991). Also, in Inner Mani there are strong semiotic parallels between the imagery of birthing and dying (ibid.). The association sparked by
toothlessness does not imply the infantilization of the elderly. In Greek rural culture, the infant, like the grandma, participates in a liminality with divinatory and
cosmological implications. With the intensification of modernity and the internalization of Western notions of the life cycle and human development both the
infant and grandma, particularly in the urban milieu, undergo a reciprocal infantilization as helpless entities.

3. The use of the present tense here does not imply the narrative strategy of the
ethnographic present, but simply replicates the style of storytelling in Greek culture. If we accept that anthropology is another form of storytelling, we must allow for indigenous forms of narration to infiltrate the ethnographic narrative.

4. See Seremetakis (1991) for a discussion of the "points" of the body as limi-
nal orifices where exchanges between the outside and inside take place.

5. For a fuller description of olive cultivation as well as the emotional and
symbolic connotations of olives and the olive tree see Seremetakis (1991).

6. See Weiner (1976) and Strathern (1988) for analogous descriptions of the personalization of matter in Melanesian contexts. However, their accounts do not explicitly focus on the link between emotions and historicization (witnessing) which is central to the understanding of exchange both in Greece and in other cultures.

7. Expressions such as "I hear the garlic" are used throughout Greece and most commonly in Crete and the Peloponnese. Dictionary definitions of the verb *akoúo* (I hear) associate it with the auditory, including literal hearing, but also receptive learning and obeying an order; the latter indicating that hearing is never passive but tied to the notion of agency. It is also tied to witnessing as in the phrase "I hear in the name of" (my name is). At issue in this article is the metaphorization of hearing in other senses such as taste and vision. This metonymic displacement violates any segmentation of the senses as discrete perceptual organs. However it cannot be translated as a generic term for perception ("encoded sensation"). This gloss would lose the inflection of methaphorical transfer from one sense to another. *Akoúo* is not a generic phrase that takes on the character of a particular sense in changing situations. To maintain this is to assume a division of the senses. To translate it as generic perception is also to maintain a Cartesian distinction between language and material experience which reduces the polysemy of sensory crossing to rhetorical word-play.

8. The naming of body parts and sensory capacities throws new light on Greek personal naming and exchange. Earlier discussions of Greek naming practices in anthropology viewed naming as the mechanical reflex of kinship rules, inheritance requirements and collective religious identity (See for instance Bialor 1967; Kenna 1976). Personal naming was understood as upholding homeostatic, atemporal or cyclical institutions; it was also primarily viewed as an ideational-linguistic practice. Alternate generational naming is supposed to assimilate the individual to the kin collective of persons who share names and eventually depersonalize those whose names are transferred to later generations. This style of naming replicates collective institutions by suppressing the passing of finite time (see, for example, Herzfeld 1982). Herzfeld added a performative element to this model by suggesting that Greek naming constructs social identity through the instrumental manipulation of rules and norms; the ultimate concern was what one "gains" from the conferral. Here, naming was associated with the rhetorical side of performance and value manipulation.

Baptismal naming has also been linked to the symbolic "resurrection" of the person whose name is transferred. But here the vernacular use of the term "resurrection" has been restricted to the theological sense of the term as an event and final outcome which preserves individual identity against death. In contrast, this paper shows that "resurrection," "raising" and "baking" are neither isolatable nor terminal events, but speak to ongoing and accumulated reciprocities, and to long term caring for the other. This is the storage and personification of the self in the other over time which cultivates, matures and individualizes the recipient through the poetic intensification of sensory memory. Personification must be distinguished from any dichotomy of the individual and the collective that informs all discussions of Greek naming (see for example Stewart 1988). Personification is the transcription of the self into alterity, *not* the recycling of identity onto a blank mimetic slate. It does not aim at producing repetitive sameness, it is instead, a thoroughly historical and historicizing process that recuperates the difference between the young and the old, the living and the dead, the past and the present. This historical sensibility, with its focus on the shifting of emotions, identity, substance and memory from one form or vessel to another, also carries with it an aesthetic sensibility for variety and multiplicity. Personification through sensory and personal naming does not lead to depersonalization but rather to the cultivation of the distinct through transformative exchange, which preserves nothing that is not first altered by being exchanged.

Thus to limit naming practices to mentalist-linguistic and instrumental formulas, is to cover with dust the sensorial, materially dense, performed poetry, *poesis* (making and imagining), of naming. Through reciprocities of naming and other modes of exchange the self is, via the senses, dispersed and transcribed in parts onto diversity and history. These issues have been discussed in length in *The Last Word* (Seremetakis, 1991).

9. The critique of descriptive realism here does not necessarily mean to say that there is no reality outside the text, but rather points to the possibility of alternative modes of describing and depicting the Real which retroactively locate realism as a cultural construct with its own historical and social specificity.

10. Colporteurs or colporters are hawkers and peddlers (originally of books, pamphlets and religious tracts). For a literary analysis of colportage, colporteurs, and their relation to spontaneous cultural montage see Bloch (1989). He associates it with ". . . the yearning for a constellation in the world, made out of esoteric and weird things, the yearning for the curious as objective quality." (Bloch, 1991: 181).

11. These characteristics distinguish colportage as defined here and by Ernst Bloch (1991), from Levi-Strauss' famous notion of *bricolage* which emphasizes the ordered placement of a serendipity of materials within a stabilized structure which then endows these elements with a classificatory order. Colportage contests discrete systems of classification.

12. Recently it has become fashionable in anthropology to criticize any tendency to exoticize as ethnocentric and romantic. However such criticism has been deployed in such a reductionist manner as to efface indigeneous fascinations with the exotic and local "romanticisms" in diverse societies which may have little to do with 19th century European predilections and their contemporary hold overs.

13. In *Ritual, Power and the Body* (Seremetakis 1993).

14. This correlates with the privatization of what is actually social memory, which is consequently removed from collective historical consciousness.

15. Marcus's discussion of "corridor talk" indexes a repressed commensality in academia since it engages unofficial practices for consuming and exchanging disciplinary knowledge.

16. See Stoller (1989), for an analogous critique of fieldwork and protocols of representation in anthropology.

17. The growing legitimacy of short-term fieldwork within anthropology merely exacerbates this situation.

References

Asad, Talal, ed. 1975. *Anthropology and the Colonial Encounter*. Atlantic Highlands: Humanities Press.

Bialor, Perry. 1967. What's In a Name? Aspects of the Social Organization of a Greek Farming Community Related to Naming Customs. *Essays in Balkan Ethnology*, W.G. Lockwood, ed. Kroeber Anthropological Society Special Publication, no. 1, pp. 95–108.

Bloch, Ernst. 1989. Better Castles in the Sky at the Country Fair and Circus, in Fairy Tales and Colportage (1959). *The Utopian Function of Art and Literature: Selected Essays*, translated by J. Zipes and F. Mecklenburg. Cambridge: MIT Press.

———. 1991. *Heritage of Our Times*. Trans. Neville and Stephen Plaice. Berkeley: University of California Press.

Buck-Morss, Susan. 1989. *The Dialectics of Seeing: Walter Benjamin and the Arcades Project*. Cambridge, Mass.: MIT Press.

Corbin, Alain. 1986. *The Foul and the Fragrant: Odor and the French Social Imagination*. New York: Berg Publishers.

Clifford, James. 1988. *The Predicament of Culture: Twentieth Century Ethnography, Literature and Art*. Cambridge, Mass.: Harvard University Press.

Crary, Jonathan. 1991. *Techniques of the Observer: On Vision and Modernity in the Nineteenth Century*. Cambridge, Mass.: MIT Press.

duBois, Page. 1988. *Sowing the Body: Psychoanalysis and Ancient Representations of Women*. Chicago: University of Chicago Press.

Fabian, Johannes. 1983. *Time and the Other: How Anthropology Makes Its Object*. New York: Columbia University Press.

Foucault, Michel. 1979. *Discipline and Punish: The Birth of the Prison*. London: Perigrin Books.

Gay, Peter. 1984. *The Education of the Senses*. Oxford: Oxford University Press.

Harvey, David. 1989. *The Condition of Postmodernity: An Inquiry into the Origins of Cultural Change*. Oxford: Blackwell.

Haviaras, Stratis. 1979. *When the Tree Sings*. New York: Simon and Schuster.

Herzfeld, Michael. 1982. When Exceptions Define the Rules: Greek Baptismal Names and the Negotiation of Identity. *Journal of Anthropological Research*, vol. xxxviii, pp. 288–302.

Kenna, Margaret. 1976. Houses, Fields and Graves: Property Rites and Ritual Obligation on a Greek Island. *Ethnology*, vol. XV, pp. 21–34.

Marcus, George. 1991. A Broad(er)side to the Canon. *Cultural Anthropology* 6 (3): 385–405.

Seremetakis, C. Nadia. 1984. The Eye of the Other. *Journal of Modern Hellenism*, vol.1, no.1, pp. 63–77.

———. 1990. The Ethics of Antiphony: The Social Construction of Pain, Gender and Power in the Southern Peloponnese. *Ethos* 18(4):481–511.

———. 1991. *The Last Word: Women, Death, and Divination in Inner Mani*. Chicago: University of Chicago Press.

———. 1993. *Ritual, Power and the Body: Historical Perspectives on the Representation of Greek Women*, edited. New York: Pella Publishing Co. (Greek Studies).

Stewart, Charles. 1988. The Role of Personal Names on Naxos, Greece. *Journal of the Anthropological Society of Oxford*, vol. xix, no. 2, pp. 151–159.

Stoller, Paul. 1989. *The Taste of Ethnographic Things: The Senses in Anthropology.* Philadelphia: University of Pennsylvania Press.

Strathern, Marilyn. 1988. *The Gender of the Gift: Problems with Women and Problems with Society in Melanesia.* Berkeley: University of California Press.

Vigarello, G. 1988. *Concepts of Cleanliness: Changing Attitudes in France since the Middle Ages.* Cambridge: Cambridge University Press.

Weiner, Annette. 1976. *Women of Value, Men of Renown: New Perspectives in Trobriand Exchange.* Austin: University of Texas Press.

4

The Cinema Screen as Prosthesis of Perception: A Historical Account

Susan Buck-Morss

"The task I am trying to achieve is above all to make you see."[1]

—D. W. Griffith

In 1907 Edmund Husserl delivered a series of lectures at Göttingin on "The Idea of Phenomenology."[2] Written midway between his major early works, *Logische Untersuchungen* (1901) and *Ideen* (1912), these short lectures explicate a philosophical project destined to become one of the most influential schools of the twentieth century.[3]

What was at stake in the project was to make evident a method of cognition that, while keeping the analysis "immanent" to the contents of consciousness, could still achieve an "absolute" and "universal" knowledge. Husserl wanted us to "see" what was essential in the experiential world within the act of perception (*Wahrnehmung*)—the thought-act in its "pure" form. Thoughts were always "thoughts of something," but their contents could be seen, he insisted, as self-given, without recourse to the objects of the natural world "out there" (the "transcendental" objects of Descartes). His was still very much the Kantian problematic; his epistemological concern remains within the long and problematic tradition of bourgeois idealism. But it is his preoccupation with the philosophical eye, his strenuous attempt to "inspect" mental acts until their essences can be purely, intuitively "seen" as absolute and non-contingent, that marks his project with a decisive difference.

The sustained metaphor of sight in his 1907 essay is as striking in its presence as it is opaque in its ability to communicate what it is that Husserl is actually up to. He performs a series of bizarre philosophical operations on the acts of perception—the famous phenomenological

45

"reductions"—which, by the principle of "epochē", or "bracketing", attempt to reach the "pure" or "reduced" objects that can be "seen" absolutely in their "immediate givenness." The first operation, the so-called "apodictic reduction," brackets out both the actual material objects of the mental act and the psychological subject that thinks (or "intends") them by this act (thereby eliminating the "natural attitude" of science). By means of the second operation, the "eidetic reduction", the reduced thought-object is itself examined phenomenologically,[4] in order to "see" the universal essences of which it is constituted.

An enormous amount of philosophical rigor is involved in these procedures. The reader of Husserl's text today, like the listener in the audience of Husserl's lectures then, must make a great intellectual effort, struggling diligently to "see" with the great philosopher these "marvelously" reduced phenomena, to have a "pure intuition" of the type his words describe. He tells us it is to be compared to the "intellectual *seeing*" described by the mystics.[5] And yet it is not medieval mysticism that provides the most accessible route to Husserl's project. If we wish to have a vision of the pure object, this "self-given," "absolute datum," which is neither physical thing nor psychological fact but (—wondrous phrase!—) an "intentionally inexistent entity",[6] we would do best to put down the text, leave the lecture, and go to the movies.

I mean this in the most exact and literal sense. For it is the everyday experience of cinema that gives us to "see," quite unpretentiously, the apodictically reduced, phenomenological object of cognition of which Husserl is speaking. If we listen to the words of Husserl, but think the cinematic image, the obscurity of phenomenology begins to dissipate before our very eyes.

Going to the movies is an "act of pure seeing"[7] if there ever was one. What is perceived in the cinema image is not a psychological fact, but a phenomenological one. It is "reduced," that is, reality is "bracketed out." The image is always an image "of something"; it is intentional, pointing to a reality beyond itself;[8] yet this transcendent reality is never "given" in the cinema images themselves, that "neither are nor genuinely contain the objects."[9] As a consequence, it is a matter of total "irrelevance"[10]—an "epistemological nullity"—whether the object "given" for perception in the cinema image actually exists. To use two early film examples: The absolutely unreal train in Méliès' *Impossible Voyage* (1904—figure 1), no less than the absolutely realistic train of Lumière's *Arrival of a Train at La Ciotat Station* (1895—figure 2), is "self-given in the strictest sense—in such a way that nothing which is meant fails to be given."[11]

Not only is the actual, or "transcendent" object "bracketed out." The subject, too, undergoes a reduction. The cinema image, although con-

FIGURE 1 Méliès, "The Impossible Voyage" (1904)

structed by particular human beings (director, camera-person, editor), is
not dependent on these or any other individual, psychological subjects
for its meaning. It is "constituted"[12] as a totally intentional act; yet it can
present us only with something perceived as "given"—allowing us "to
ignore the ego, or at least abstract from "our psychological selves"[13] (figure 3). Pudovkin, trying to argue for the cameraman's infinite power, declared first that the spectator sees "only that which the director desires to
show him," but was forced immediately to add: "or, more correctly put,
that which the director himself sees in the action concerned"[14]—implying
the director's total *dependence* on the outside world. This is the paradox
of montage. That which it shows us is both given (in the pieces of film),
and constructed (in the juxtaposition that gives these pieces meaning).
"Neither a component of the ego nor of the contemporary world," it is
"absolute data grasped in purely immanent 'seeing,'"[15] in which we "directly inspect the unity of cognition and its object."[16] It is cognition that
"sees itself."[17]

In a close-up of Pudovkin's "Mother" (figure 4) we automatically see
the "eidetically reduced," pure phenomenon of grief. It was not always
so. The audiences of early cinema—contemporaries of the audiences of

FIGURE 2   Lumière, "Arrival of a Train at La Ciotat Station" (1895)

Husserl's lecture—were at first incapable of making the kind of phenomenological reductions Husserl describes. We are told that when "a huge
'severed' head smiled at the public for the first time there was panic in
the cinema."[18] "As the first close-ups appeared on the screen the specta-
tors stomped and cried: 'Show us their feet!'"[19] Viewers only gradually
adapted to the cinema screen.

Husserl does not speak about cinema, that brand new invention of his
generation. He in no way *intended* to describe such a historically specific
cognitive experience. His goal was just the opposite—absolute, pure, universal knowledge (the traditional goal of bourgeois idealism). Why, then,
attempt to argue that phenomenological philosophy finds its prototype
("Urform," to use Walter Benjamin's term) in going to the movies? On
the one hand, I am making a philosophical point. By asking you to "see"
within Husserl's pure philosophical categories the very impure technico-
material realities of his era, I am suggesting, *contra* Husserl, that truth is
*un*intentional. The objective, historically transient reality which he wants
to bracket *out* of the cogitatio penetrates precisely into that realm of "reduced" mental acts where he thought himself most secure.[20] On the other
hand, I am making an argument about cinema, and about the *screen as
prosthesis*. The surface of the cinema screen functions as an artificial organ
of cognition. The prosthetic organ of the cinema screen does not merely
duplicate human cognitive perception, but changes its nature.

In regard to both time and space, the effect of the techniques of cinema is to pry perception loose from the larger world of which it is a part, subject it to extreme temporal[21] and spatial[22] condensation, and hold it suspended, floating in a seemingly autonomous set of dimensions. Lotman speaks of the temporality of film as exclusively the present.[23] Yet it is always a simulated present, because there is a temporal and spatial gap between the recording of the perception and its being "seen." The fact that, in Husserl's words, it is a matter of "irrelevance" whether what is perceived is real or not, is due to this gap. The cinema image is the recorded, kinetic trace of an absence. It is the present image of an object that has either disappeared or perhaps never existed.[24] In short, it is the form—one of the Ur-forms—of the simulacrum.

My claim is not ontological in the strong sense. I am not arguing that the cognitive prosthesis of the cinema, inherently, has only one way of being. The metaphysics of early cinema developed within a particular set of historical and cultural determinants, which is to say that it could have

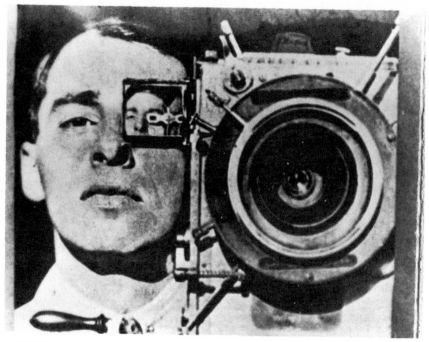

FIGURE 3   Vertov, "The Man with a Movie Camera" (1920)

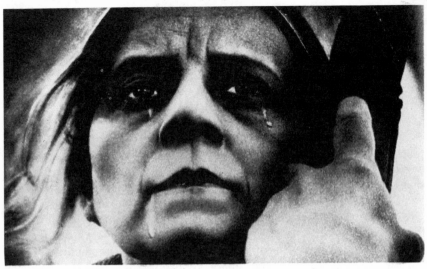

FIGURE 4   Pudovkin, "Mother" (1926)

developed otherwise. In fact, particularly after World War II, avant-garde
and experimental cinema became preoccupied with making the cinematic prosthesis itself the object of the film experience, in order to expose
its historically developed metaphysics. Indeed, directors attempted to
fight against that metaphysics by means of cinema's own techniques. But
what fascinated the first filmmakers was precisely the fact that it *could* be
a matter of indifference whether what is perceived is real or not. On the
screen the moving images have a present meaning despite the absence of
corporeal bodies,[25] which thereby becomes a matter of indifference. What
counts is the simulacrum, not corporeal object behind it. In the prosthetic
cognition of the cinema, the difference between documentary and fiction
is thus effaced. Of course we still "know" that they are different. But they
inhabit the surface of the screen as cognitive equivalents. Both the real
event and the staged event are absent. Their appearance of being present
is equally simulated. Both are constructed, or "constituted" by an intend-
ing consciousness, dependent on the same filmic principles of shooting
and montage for their meaning. As Kuleshov showed us, it is not the actuality of Muzekin's grimace that is meaningful, but what shots come before and after. In Baudrillard's terms, the code takes over and dominates
the meaning: "the code no longer refers back to any subjective or objective 'reality' but to its own logic."[26]

Once this reduction takes place, once the simulated imminence of the
reduced cinema object is the source of meaning, then a certain kind of
violence becomes possible. I am speaking not only of the violence of

framing and montage that cuts into reality, dismembers the body and slashes through every aspect of reality's continuum in the process of constructing the image. I am speaking of the violence of the prosthetic perception itself.

A New Kind of Violence

D. W. Griffith in *The Birth of a Nation* (1915) created a long sequence on the hostilities of the U.S. Civil War. Several years later, toward the end of World War I, he visited the French front to make a propaganda film. He declared that he was "very disappointed with the reality of the battlefield."[27] He retreated to England where he created synthetically the battles taking place across the Channel. His film *Hearts of the World* (1918) was completed in Hollywood on a private ranch. Virilio tells us: "it was a big success in the United States and had considerable impact on public opinion."[28]

Modern warfare cannot be comprehended as raw experience. Like many of the realities of modernity, war needs the prosthetic organ of the cinema screen in order to be "seen." Virilio declares outright: "War is cinema and cinema is war."[29] We do not need to go that far to realize that what we know as war can no longer be separated from its cinematic representation. This is not only true for the public. No modern general, no bomber pilot, can do without the simulated perception of the kinetic image. The point is that certain events can only take place on the prosthetic surface of the screen. Certain phenomena can only exist within the dimensions of cinematic perception. Walter Benjamin believed that the city could only truly be experienced this way, and of course the crowded streets and public spaces of modern cities (Paris, Berlin, Moscow) became a privileged object of early film construction. Pudovkin wrote that in order to receive "a clear and definite impression" of a street demonstration, the observer must view it from the roof of a house, a first-floor window, and mingling with the crowd—a simultaneity of points of view that only the mobile camera and montage can provide.[30]

Tied to all these examples—war, the city, street demonstrations—and key to their dependency on the screen as prosthesis of cognition, is that they are phenomena of the crowd, or "mass." The Russian philosopher Valery Podoroga has argued that the mass can *only* inhabit the simulated, indefinite space of the screen. Cinema creates an imaginable space where a mass body exists that can exist nowhere else. "No reality could stand the intensity of the mass shown in cinema."[31] Eisenstein showed us in his film images the crowd of people as a composite form, a "protoplasmic being in the process of becoming," a "flow of violence" that fills the screen, extending human bodies to the "limit of their expressivity."[32]

Even more than the civil war newsreels of 1918–21, Eisenstein's feature films—*Strike, October, Battleship Potemkin*—gave an experience of the mass that became "characteristic of the era." Against initial resistance of audiences not yet used to the new cinematic prosthesis, Eisenstein tried to make visible such abstract realities as capital, class oppression, and, most especially, the mass as the collective agent of the new historical events. The particular characteristics of the screen as a cognitive organ enabled audiences not only to "see" this new collective protagonist, but (through eidetic reduction) to "see" the idea of the unity of the revolutionary people, the collective sovereignty of the masses, the idea of international solidarity, the idea of revolution itself.

Indeed, it is doubtful whether the Soviet experience would have been possible without cinema, and Lenin—a contemporary of Husserl—turned out to be more right than he knew when he called it the most important of the arts. The building of a Soviet state after his death was, like the revolutionary struggle, a process that needed the cinema world in which to *be*. Vertov's *A Sixth of the World* (1926), which synthesized old newsreels and new material, was commissioned by Gorstog (the Government Trade Agency) for international circulation,[33] but its impact was greatest domestically, within the Soviet Union, where it gave a simulated immanence to the idea of "socialism in one country" by introducing a pleased public to the myriad of ethnic types as the new Soviet "we."

The Soviet Union as simulacrum! But it was not alone. Precisely in the same period, the United States, laden with new immigrants, was promoting a melting-pot ideology that relied on the silent cinema as it could rely on no other cultural institution. Churches, theatres, schools, holiday rituals, political organizations all embodied specific linguistic and ethnic traditions. Hollywood movies that "screened *out* the past" became *the* culture of mass assimilation. Earlier, sympathetic depictions of working-class struggles (e.g., the shocking violence against the demonstrating workers by the state militia in Griffith's *Intolerance*) were superceded by euphoric visions of assimilation: In John Ford's film *The Iron Horse* (1925) the building of the transcontinental railroad symbolizes national unity among the Polish, Chinese and Italian workers who "can put aside labor conflict for the great opportunities of industrial America."[34] For the USSR, it was being part of the same historical struggle that created the unity of the masses. For the U.S., it was being part of the same territorial space. But for both, with increasing technical realism, the cinematic prosthesis shaped the political imaginary.

Hollywood created a new mass hero, the individualized composite of the "star." It can be argued that, like Eisenstein's protoplasmic mass, Hollywood's new mass-being, the movie star, could only exist in the "super-space" (Podoroga) of the cinematic screen. Often, and increasingly female, the star was a sublime and simulated corporeality. Close-ups of parts of her/his body—mouth, eyes, legs, heaving breast—filled the screen in monstrous proportions. S/he was an awesome aesthetic spectacle, like a massive church icon, surrounded by the symbolic clutter of the objects of conspicuous consumption. The Hollywood star, with a new, non-ethnic name, and rhinoplastic surgery on nose and orthodontic surgery on teeth, fulfilled her/his mass function by obliterating the idio-syncratic irregularities of the natural body. The star was an article of mass consumption, whose multiplying image guaranteed the infinite re-production of the same. The deeper the camera penetrated, the more it gave back a universal visage, whose features (like those of Eisenstein's crowd) became surface, ornamental lines—contours on the screen. Of course, a true star had to have a particular, identifiable "look." But this was the opposite of the accidental luminescent quality of the natural face. It was a standardized image, a cliché (a *pontif*). Like an advertising logo, it could be instantly identifiable as the mark of presence of an absence. This image, this mark of "presence," was not a reference to the individ-ual, actual person, the natural body of the star. Rather, that body was itself a sign; its meaning was erotic desire. If the Soviet screen provided a prosthetic experience of collective power, the Hollywood screen pro-vided a prosthetic experience of collective desire.

In Hollywood movies, class movement meant social mobility, the rev-olution was sexual, the decisive events were marriage and divorce. But the "star" was as much an indigenous inhabitant of the cinema screen as the revolutionary mass. Both, as synthetic corporealities, were simulacra, "given" as an object of cognition only on the surface of the screen. More-over, both gave back to the viewing audience a perception of the mass-as-image which they internalized. The superspace of the screen and its superinhabitants were taken over as a part of their own cognitive func-tioning. The crowd in a movie theatre not only experiences the masses. It has a "mass" experience. The movie audience is not an assembly of indi-vidual viewers. It is *one* viewer, infinitely reproduced.

A New Kind of Subject

Marcel Pagnol has written:

A theatre audience of a thousand cannot all sit in the same place, and so one can say that none of them sees the same play. [. . .] Cinema solves this problem, however, because what each member of the audience sees from anywhere in the room (or in a country, where there is an audience of mil-lions) is the exact picture taken by the camera. If Charlie Chaplin looks at the lens, his picture will look straight at anyone who sees it, whether they are on the left or the right, upstairs or downstairs. . . . So there is not just an audience of a thousand (or millions if all the cinemas are included); *now there is only one audience which sees and hears exactly as the camera and microphone do.*[35]

Intersubjectivity presented an enormous problem for Husserl. The pure act of seeing could be comprehended as universal only if it was "seen" by all other minds, not just his own.[36] In the solitude of his study, Husserl struggled against the problem of solopsism. How could he be sure that the phenomenologically reduced object was intersubjectively universal, "evident" in the same way to all? Precisely this guarantee is supplied by the cinema eye. Thus in cinema-experience, the problem of intersubjective verification does not emerge. Mass audiences testify empirically to the cinema cognition as a universal experience, eliminating any need for trying to posit, through philosophical arguments, a transcendental subjectivity.

The standardization of mass cognition substitutes for *a priori* universality. There is a political danger here. If, from the start, the subject of the cognitive act is a collective subject, then cognition cannot escape conformism. If everyone has the "same" perception in the cinematic experience, that sameness has the power to simulate universality or "truth." We can make a historical comparison. As Jürgen Habermas has made us aware, the bourgeois public sphere was first conceived as one of critical debate between individuals (they were white, property-holding males) who appealed to the universality of reason to construct a legitimating consensus:

> Historically, the polemical claim of this kind of rationality was developed, in conjunction with the critical public debate among private people, against the reliance of princely authority on secrets of state.[37]

The medium of this debate was the printed word—books, political pamphlets, newspapers, and the "audience" assembled in reading rooms and coffee houses, in settings where collective "education" allowed the public debate to continue. It is significant that the political imaginary of the nineteenth century was formed by the perception of a national political collective, a community of readers of the mass-produced press who had a shared language, and were hence potential participants in the national debate.[38]

The twentieth-century collective, which constructs its identity on the basis of the image rather than the word, is, at least potentially, a truly international community, as the producers and distributors of the first silent films were well aware. This is the political advantage of the cinema as a prosthesis of cognition. But if that collective is one of conformism rather than consensus, if uniformity replaces universality, it opens the door to tyranny. If "truths" are universal because they are experienced in common rather than perceived in common because they are universal, then the cinematic prosthesis becomes an organ of power, and cognition becomes indoctrination. When the mass audience has a sense of immediate identity with the cinema screen, and perception in itself becomes consensus, the space for intersubjective, critical debate and discussion disappears.

Nervous System: Hyper-Sensation—Anaesthetized Body

Although the infinite reproducibility of cinematic experience did not depend on the audience being located in one place, the sense of the audience as a massified "one" became magnified with the construction of the palatial movie houses built in both the United States (where they replaced the amusement park nickelodeons and old vaudeville theatres) and the Soviet Union (where post-revolutionary audiences had been introduced to the movies in the cinema cars of agitprop trains). These monumental structures, built to reflect the height of architectural good taste, seated upward of 6,000 persons. The simultaneity of sensory stimulation that such mass showings provided was something brand new. This needs to be kept in mind in order to appreciate the enormous intensity of the cinematic experience, and its potential capacity for a brand new euphoria of mass communication—or should I say mass communion? The archaic meaning of the word "prosthesis" is the place in the Eastern orthodox Church where the Eucharist table is prepared. What is different in these prosthetic experiences relates to the nervous system. The religious communal experience is one of bliss. The cinematic communal experience is one of shock.

Cognition is a physical as well as an intellectual function. If we consider the cinema screen as a prosthetic organ of the senses, then one characteristic strikes us as paramount. Exposed to the sensual shock of the cinema, the nervous system is subject to a double, and seemingly paradoxical modification: On the one hand there is an extreme heightening of the senses, a hypersensitivity of nervous stimulation. On the other, there is a dulling of sensation, a numbing of the nervous system that is tantamount to corporeal anaesthetization.

The simultaneously hypersensitized and anaesthetized mass body that is the subject of the cinematic experience is held in this paradoxical situation by the same simulated immanence that describes the reduced cinema object. Precisely because the bodies of the beings that inhabit the screen are absent, cinema viewers can perform certain cognitive operations that would otherwise be humanly intolerable—intolerable for the cinema bodies as well as the cinema viewers. The prosthetic organ of the cinema assures that both are anaesthetized, because both are absent from the scene.

Bodily absence sets the stage for the other pole, a heightened intensification of the senses. The techniques of framing, close-up and montage are powerful instruments for the intensification of the senses. They expose the nerve endings to extreme stimulation from the most shocking physical sensations: violence and torture, the terrifying and catastrophic, the tantalizing and erotic. Walter Benjamin, comparing the cameraman and painter, uses as an analogy the difference between surgeon and magician. The magician, like the painter, "maintains in his work a natural distance from reality"; in magic healing, he maintains that distance between the patient and himself. The surgeon, like the cameraman, "does exactly the reverse": abstaining from facing the patient "man to man," he radically diminishes the natural space between persons in order to penetrate deeply into the body and move "with caution among the organs."[39] Benjamin considered the representation of reality by the film "incomparably more significant than that of the painter," due to the technical penetration of reality of which it is capable.[40] This cognitive gain did not come without a price.

If we compare the painter's canvas to the cinema screen, Benjamin's analogy is sustained. Let me refer to Helena Petrovskaya's work on Goya and Picasso. She points out that both artists depicted violence (war in Mexico, The Spanish Civil War) in a way that sustains the shock of pain, the human anguish of the events. "Violence dashes out in a forward thrust"; it leaps out from the canvas and assails the viewer, "to deprive him for good of an estranged beholding gaze."[41] But it is precisely the "estranged, beholding gaze" that the anaesthetizing screen allows, in order that the surgical procedures of the camera can dissect reality and expose it to our heightened powers of perception.

Virilio writes: "Numerous veterans from the 1914–18 war have said to me that although they killed enemy soldiers, at least they did not see whom they were killing. . . ."[42] This merciful blindness is denied the movie-goer. Cinema, as Kracauer writes, "insists on making visible what is commonly drowned in inner agitation."[43] Sitting, facing forward, in the darkened theatre, totally subjected to what Podoroga calls the "tearless eye" of the camera, the viewer is bombarded by physical and psychic shock, but feels no pain. And as part of a mass audience, his or her shock is absorbed simultaneously by thousands—ultimately, on repeated show-ings, it will be millions. For each of these millions of viewers, the motor reaction to stimulus is suppressed. The shocking, hyper-sensory cinema-events are absorbed passively, severing the connection between percep-tion and muscular innervation. In the cinema we endure the most erotic provocations, the most brutal acts of violence, but we do nothing. The continuum between cognition and action is snapped. Even if we are mo-tivated by a cinema experience to act in a certain way in the outside world, the delay in response changes its nature, from a metonymic reac-tion (stimulus A causes response B) to a metaphoric or mimetic one: con-fronting a similar event or experience, we act *like* the movie heroine or hero, in order to be seen as acting in a certain (cinematic) way.

Feminist theoreticians of cinema have made us aware of the violence of the gaze itself. The movie camera, and the audience with it, dehuman-izes erotic perception by reifying the screen body, which is displayed in all its intimacy as a public object for specular enjoyment. The cinematic perspective has been seen by those theorists as inherently violent, and the gaze identified with phallocentrism, that is, masculine power. The psychic economy of the gaze is not simple: Lacan observed that there is a difference between the "look" of desire and the (potentially punishing) "gaze" of power—under the gaze of power, the look of desire experi-ences shame. In the cinema viewer, these are conflated, setting up an am-biguity of affect. This ambiguity is compounded by the ambivalent posi-tion of the viewer, who both shares with the camera the all-powerful ocular appropriation of reality, and, as passive viewer, relinquishes all power of corporeal response. Even the action of booing or applause that could interrupt the live performance is denied to the movie-viewer. All kinetic activity is reserved for the "objectified" screen-bodies—who are as anaesthetized to the audience reaction as the latter is to the spectacle of their bodily pain. And yet, despite the fact that they feel no pain, the screen bodies remain vulnerable to the pure, reduced, and intrusive bru-tality of the gaze.

This psychic ambivalence is further complicated when we consider our earlier point, that the audience-as-mass is viewing *itself* upon the screen. The libidinal circuit that results from all these complexities does not lend itself to easy generalizations. Key to its conceptual understand-ing, however, is the psychological dynamics of sado-masochism—in the viewers' attitude not only toward the corporeality of the Other, but to the corporeality of themselves as well.

Podoroga has exposed the "cinematic metaphysics" of Eisenstein in similar terms. For Eisenstein, "human bodies became experiments for graphic representations."[44] He stretched the human expressivity to the limits. Through a "tailoring of the body," he destroyed its natural organic form. Through the "deep and painful transformation of the actor's face," he achieved, as pure line, the phenomenological expression of pain. But for Eisenstein, even laughter can become an occasion for stretching the face to the limit. Podoroga calls this Eisenstein's "madness." He argues that ordinarily we do not experience pure emotion, and this helps us to be sane. When pure emotion enters us, we turn into clinical patients. In Eisenstein's images, there is a predominance of the aesthetic in cognition—an aesthetics of the line, and of surface pattern. Now, this aestheticization of cognition is a tendency for which the viewers are predisposed. As an anaesthetized mass body, the movie audience is absolutely prepared for an experience of "disinterested interest," to cite Kant's definition of the aesthetic attitude.

In keeping with this aestheticization of cognition, Eisenstein became obsessed with eliminating from the image exactly that which other movie-makers (Vertov, for example) considered the essence of cinema: the accidental. In 1939, he wrote that he wanted actors to exert "self control . . . to the millimeter of movement."[45] Leyda reports Eisenstein's directions to actors: "With both skilled and unskilled actors, he first solves their physical problems: What are my torso and limbs and head doing at this point? How will my movement over to there be managed?"[46] There is an uncanny similarity to the disembodied relationship between consciousness and its physical self as described by Husserl in *Ideen*, where he discusses the corporeal body as the "turning point" between subject and object. Husserl explains:

> If I cut my finger with a knife, then a physical body is split by the driving into it of a wedge, the fluid contained in it trickles out, etc. Likewise, the physical thing, "my Body," . . . can become electrically charged through contact with an electric current; . . . and one can elicit noises from it by striking it.[47]

It is worth noting that Husserl was as obsessively concerned with eliminating the accidental from his philosophy as Eisenstein was from his films. Theirs is the same impulse, the same kind of violence, achieved through the abstraction of pure and reduced cognition.

There is a cinema image that allows us to "see" the elements of this cognitive violence. The scene is from the movie *Julia* (1977, directed by Fred Zinnemann), a commercial film based on Lillian Hellman's memoir, *Pentimento*. It takes place in Austria during the Nazi era. The war is lost; the Reich is endangered. A doctor, who worked contentedly on the Nazi medical experimentations, decides to take his life. He swallows cyanide, picks up a mirror, and gazes in it at his own convulsions, trying to "see" the invisible moment of his death.

Notes

1. D. W. Griffith, in an interview from 1913, cited in Siegrfried Kracauer, *Theory of Film: The Redemption of Physical Reality* (New York: Oxford University Press, 1960), p. 41.

2. Husserl, "The Idea of Phenomenology," trans. William P. Alston and George Nakhnikian (The Hague: Martinus Nijhoff, 1964).

3. Husserl's influence on Heidegger was direct and decisive; his philosophy has preoccupied continental thinkers as diverse as Adorno and Derrida, Habermas and Levinas, Gadamer and Sartre. The movement of phenomenology is presently institutionalized on a global level. Under the leadership of N. Matroschilova, Institute of Philosophy, Moscow, it has a strong and vital branch within the former Soviet Union.

4. "[P]erception itself stands open to my inspection" (Husserl, "The Idea of Phenomenology," p. 24).

5. Husserl, "The Idea of Phenomenology," p. 50. This is in opposition to discursive knowledge.

6. Husserl, "The Idea of Phenomenology," p. xiv.

7. Husserl, "The Idea of Phenomenology," p. 23.

8. "Cognitive mental processes (and this belongs to their essence) have an *intentio*, they refer to something, they are related in this or that way to an object. This activity of relating itself to an object belongs to them even if the object itself does not" (Husserl, "The Idea of Phenomenology," p. 43).

9. Husserl, "The Idea of Phenomenology," p. 56.

10. Husserl, "The Idea of Phenomenology," p. 43.

11. Husserl, "The Idea of Phenomenology," p. 49. The cinema image is "an absolutely given, pure phenomenon in the phenomenological sense, renouncing anything transcendent" (ibid., p. 35).

12. The perceived objects "are not mental acts" but they are "nevertheless constituted, and come to be given in such acts. It is only as so constituted that they display themselves as what they are. But is this not an absolute marvel? And where does this constituting of objects begin and where does it end?" (Husserl, "The Idea of Phenomenology," p. 57).

13. Husserl, "The Idea of Phenomenology," p. 34.

14. V. I. Pudovkin, *Film Technique and Film Acting* [1929], trans. Ivor Montagu (New York: Grove Press, 1978).

15. Husserl, "The Idea of Phenomenology," p. 35. "Thus at this point we speak of such absolute data; even if these data are related to objective actuality via their intentions, their intrinsic character is *within* them; nothing is assumed concerning *the existence or non-existence of actuality*. And so we have dropped anchor on the shore of phenomenology [. . .] (ibid).

16. Husserl, "The Idea of Phenomenology," p. 30.

17. See Husserl, "The Idea of Phenomenology," p. 28.

18. Bela Balazs, cited in Jurij Lotman, *Semiotics of Cinema*, trans. Mark E. Suino (Ann Arbor, Michigan Slavic Contributions No. 5, 1976), p. 29.

19. Ivor Montagu, cited in Lotman, *Semiotics of Cinema*, p. 29.

20. This, incidentally, parallels Theodor Adorno's philosophical understanding

of materialism as "immanent criticism" by showing that phenomenology's insights are determined by those very specifics of the material and historical world which so threaten the phenomenological search for pure knowledge. Hence, idealism unintentionally expresses historical and material truth.

21. As Gilles Deleuze has pointed out, it was Henri Bergson who first articulated the particularity of cinema temporality with his concept of "duration" (*durée*), as opposed to the formal category of divisible, measurable time. What is quite remarkable from our point of view is that Bergson developed his conception of "durée" in his book *Creative Evolution*, published in the exact same year (1907) as Husserl's essay "The Idea of Phenomenology." Like Husserl, Bergson had no intention of seeing cinema as the prototype of his new conception. In fact, in *Matter and Memory* (1896), Bergson had equated the formal, divisible time with "cinematic illusion." Deleuze points out that the cinema camera had not yet abandoned the fixed point of view. Once the camera became mobile, the concept of *durée* was an absolutely accurate description of the new image-movement that characterized temporality in the cinema. (See Gilles Deleuze, *Cinema*, vol. 1: *The Movement Image*, trans. Hugh Tomlinson [Minneapolis: University of Minnesota Press, 1986], Chapters 1 and 2).

22. "Let us suppose that in a certain place we are photographic a certain object. Then, in a quite different place, we film people looking at this object. We edit the whole thing, alternating the image of the object and the image of the people who are looking at it. In "The Project of Engineer Prite," I show people looking at electric pylons in this way. It was then that I made an accidental discovery: thanks to montage, it is possible to create, so to speak, a new geography, a new place of action. It is possible to create in this way new relations between the objects, the nature, the people and the progress of the film" (Lev Vladimirovitch Kuleshov, "The Origins of Montage," *Cinema in Revolution*, eds. Luda and Jean Schnitzer and Marcel Martin, trans. David Robinson [London: Secker & Warburg, 1973], p. 68).

23. Lotman, *Semiotics of Cinema*, p. 77.

24. "What I think was much more interesting [than the creation of new geographies, see above note 22] was the creation of a woman who had never existed. I did this experiment with my students. I shot a scene of a woman at her toilette: She did her hair, made up, put on her stockings and shoes and dress. . . . I filmed the face, the head, the hair, the hands, the legs, the feet of different women, but I edited them as if it was all one woman, and, thanks to the montage, I succeeded in creating a woman who did not exist in reality, but only in the cinema" (Kuleshov, *Cinema in Revolution*, p. 70).

25. It "is, and remains as long as it lasts, something absolute, something here and now [. . .]" (Husserl, "The Idea of Phenomenology," p. 24).

26. Jean Baudrillard, *The Mirror of Production*, trans. Mark Poster (St. Louis: Telos Press, 1975), p. 127.

27. Cited, Paul Virilio, *War and Cinema: The Logistics of Perception*, trans. Patrick Camiller (London: Verso, 1989), p. 15.

28. Virilio, *War and Cinema*, p. 15.

29. Virilio, *War and Cinema*, p. 26.

30. Pudovkin, cited in Kracauer, *Theory of Film*, p. 51.

31. Valery Podoroga, "Sergei Eisenstein," presentation at Dubrovnik, October 1990 (forthcoming, Duke University Press).

32. Ibid (Podoroga).

33. Jay Leyda, *Kino: A History of the Russian and Soviet Film* (New York: Collier Books, 1973), p. 200.

34. See Larry May, *Screening out the Past: The Birth of Mass Culture and the Motion Picture Industry* (Chicago: The University of Chicago Press, 1980), p. 215.

35. Marcel Pagnol, cited in Paul Virilio, *War and Cinema: The Logistics of Perception*, trans. Patrick Camiller (London: Verso, 1989), p. 39.

36. "Exact scientific determination wants objective truth and this means intersubjective truth comprehensible for all thinking subjects" (Ludwig Landgrabe, *The Phenomenology of Edmund Husserl: Six Essays*, ed., Donn Welton [Ithaca: Cornell University Press, 1981], p. 36).

37. Jürgen Habermas, *The Structural Transformation of the Public Sphere: An Inquiry into a Category of Bourgeois Society*, trans. Thomas Burger (Cambridge, Mass.: The MIT Press, 1989), p. 53.

38. See Benedict Anderson, *Imagined Communities: Reflections on the Origin and Spread of Nationalism* (London: Verso, 1983).

39. Walter Benjamin, *Illuminations*, trans. Harry Zohn (New York: Schocken Books, 1969), p. 233.

40. Ibid.

41. E. V. Petrovskaya, "On the Event of War in Art: Concerning the Problem of Perceptual Violence," presentation at Dubrovnik, Oct. 1990.

42. Virilio, *War and Cinema*, p. 14.

43. Kracauer, *Theory of Film*, p. 53.

44. Valery Podoroga, "Sergei Eisenstein."

45. Kracauer, *Theory of Film*, p. 96.

46. Jay Leyda (cited from the diary of his witnessed years), *Kino: A History of the Russian and Soviet Film*, p. 334.

47. Edmund Husserl, *Ideas Pertaining to a pure phenomenology and to a phenomenological philosophy*, Book 2, trans. Richard Rojcewic and Andre Schuwer (Boston: Kluwer Academic Publishers, 1989), p. 168.

References

Anderson, Benedict. 1983. *Imagined Communities: Reflections on the Origin of Nationalism.* London: Verso.

Baudrillard, Jean. 1975. *The Mirror of Production.* Trans. Mark Poster. St. Louis: Telos Press.

Benjamin, Walter. 1969. *Illuminations.* Trans. Harry Zohn. New York: Schocken Books.

Deleuze, Gilles. 1986. *Cinema, vol. 1: The Movement Image.* Trans. Hugh Tomlinson. Minneapolis: University of Minnesota Press.

Habermas, Jürgen. 1989. *The Structural Transformation of the Public Sphere: An Inquiry into a Category of Bourgeois Society.* Trans. Thomas Burger. Cambridge, Mass.: MIT Press.

Husserl, Edmund. 1964. "The Idea of Phenomenology." Trans. William P. Alston and George Nakhnikian. The Hague: Martinus Nijhoff.

Kracauer, Siegfried. 1960. *Theory of Film: The Redemption of Physical Reality*. New York: Oxford University Press.

Kuleshov, Vladimirovitch. 1973. "The Origins of Montage." Cinema in Revolution. Luda and Jean Schnitzer and Marcel Martin, eds. Trans. David Robinson. London: Secker & Warburg.

Landgrabe, Ludwig. 1981. *The Phenomenology of Edmund Husserl: Six Essays*. Donn Weltoon, ed. Ithaca: Cornell University Press.

Leyda, Jay. 1973. *Kino: A History of the Russian and Soviet Film*. New York: Collier Books.

Lotman, Jurij. 1976. *Semiotics of Cinema*. Trans. Mark E. Suino. Ann Arbor: Michigan Slavic Contributions, no. 5.

Pudovkin, V. I. 1978. *Film Technique and Film Acting*. Trans. Ivor Montagu. New York: Grove Press.

Virilio, Paul. 1989. *War and Cinema: The Logistics of Perception*. Trans. Patrick Camiller. London: Verso.

5

On the Move: The Struggle for the Body in Sweden in the 1930s

Jonas Frykman

Power comes from below; that is, there is no binary and all-encompassing opposition between rulers and ruled at the root of all power relations, and serving as a general matrix—no such duality extending from the top down and reacting on more and more limited groups to the very depths of the social body. One must suppose rather that the manifold relationships of force that take shape and come into play in the machinery of production, in families, limited groups, and institutions, are the basis for the wide-range effects of cleavage that run through the social body as a whole (Foucault 1978:94).

Modernity as Swedish Mentality

In their analysis of social change in Sweden, several researchers in recent years have returned to that remarkable jump in the history of our century: How did it come about that one of the more marginal states in Europe in the nineteenth century, with a mainly agrarian economy, serious problems in feeding its people, and massive emigration, was transformed in less than a generation into a modern, successful nation? The change was not only about peace, the development of industry, power stations, mining, and logging, but also a question of how people's way of life and orientation were modernized in a radical manner. The large process of socialization which transformed "peasants into Swedes," to paraphrase Eugen Weber's expression, implied that national identity was wed to modernity (see Frykman 1991, Nilsson 1991). Modernity was nationalized and became Swedishness (Löfgren 1991). Being Swedish meant practicing how to look forward. When ethnologists today portray the social character of the Swede, they tend to invoke such classical modernist qualities as rationalism, industriousness, and a readiness to break away (Daun 1989).[1] Without this mental and physical readiness, the modernization of society would not have been possible. But how did it arise?

National identity has been discussed in recent times as a cultural or even narrative construction. The "imagined community" described by Benedict Anderson (1983) is one such narrative, which has given a desti- nation and a meaning to the journey undertaken by those who have been thrown out of fixed relations and have been given a taste of what it means to break away. Only the future promises stability, and the present is a resting-place on the way there—the dream of a future country is something to read on the journey. When people are torn out of their given position in a hierarchical totality, national ideology is suitable as an ideo- graphic compass. It gives identity in return for a minimum of obligations (Dumont 1986). In that respect modernity and nationality are siblings within the same radical 19th century family.

However, analyses within history and anthropology have yet to de- velop ideas about how people create a national identity in the practice of everyday life. National identities have often been considered as part of a "fabrication" design by the élites or the ruling classes. Citizens within a state were thought to be brought up as members of a nation. Who were the parents and for what abominable tasks were the children trained? To unveil the true nature of hegemonic nationalism, was, during the 70s and 80s, a way of analyzing processes of domestication or discipline—and getting rid of "false conciousness."

Studies of today's Sweden show extensively how ethnic and national categories are used by people in everyday encounters, how identities are negotiated and reorganized. The geographical and intellectual mobility offered by modern society has meant that people have been trained to interact in a multitude of everyday life situations. The discourse on national identity has become possible because people perceive differences— Swedishness and Danishness are defined in terms of mutual contrasts. There are quite a lot of Others to identify oneself against. Still this seems to be closely tied to the experience of life within modernity.

A wide variety of popular uses of these concepts is discernible here.[2] But is this really a process that has just begun now at the end of the cen- tury? Were people effectively indoctrinated before or did some kind of definition of national identity also take place in everyday life? Did it also come "from below" as well as from above?

The least cultivated field of research appears to be the discussion of how senses and dispositions are formed in a sort of everyday micro- physics. Is it possible to single out a series of behaviors, emotions, and habits—a way of knowing and being—without falling back into psycho- logical reasoning about an inherited, traditional, or socialized character? Could this be done without demonstrating how the molding of the senses is the prime target of the state when it comes to establish a relation of power and dominance?[3] Is it possible to look at how people did constitute a new identity by way of *acting*, and exploring their own potentials?

On the one hand we have the scholarly tradition of studying how identity is the outcome of discourses of power and how it is constituted in a process of discipline, civilization or domination. This leaves little room for experience, for sentiments, for the constitution of identity as a reflexive project. On the other hand we have the more romantic tradition of describing cultural identity as something formed and performed in the local or little world in spite of the surrounding turbulence and the supposedly futile efforts of the state or ruling classes. On the exotic fringe of ethnography, descriptions have been produced, and are still being produced, of how identity based on community and tradition is passed on between individuals and generations as if it was some elusive substance. Today research into ethnicity and nationality has produced a sort of rampant "tribalism," where people try to find a complete picture of the modal personality, mentality, or character of a particular culture. Researchers' concepts of "culture" or "national identity" have been taken seriously and made not into analytical instruments but nouns. In ethnology "culture" today is used as a verb, something always in the making (Ehn, Frykman & Löfgren 1993).

This paper then, is an attempt to show how cultural identity, can be seen as a process, as something "produced simultaneously in many different locales of activity by many different agents for many different purposes" (Marcus 1992:315) and how the modernization of the body and the senses can be described as a process containing experience, discovery as well as instruction. In more concrete terms, my intention is to discuss how Swedish bodies—senses, feelings, and habits—were formed in an intensive interplay between state policies, class interests, everyday circumstances, and historically given cultural structures in the 1930s. This will be done by using gymnastics and the outdoor life of the time as the point of departure.

The description has two important front lines. On one front I challenge the discussion of dispositions as *characteristics* and totalities or socialized identities instead of actions, contrasts, confrontation, and malleability. The other front opposes analyses which assume that processes of this kind emanate from some center. As an ethnologist, I find it more natural to see how the power to define the body is a process initiated from below, as well as from the sides, from history, and from the future. Willingness to break away is tested and realized in the practical actions of everyday life, so everyday practice ought to provide some foundation for the study of how cultural identity is created. Although ethnology has concentrated on analyzing the organization of everyday life, there has been little consideration that this is the place where societal power is constituted (Lindqvist 1988).

The Quest for Truth

Every change in society takes on a physical form. Classes, genders, and cultural groups emphasize their distinctness in corporal terms, and exactly the same is true of epochs. In the way of moving the body, guarding its boundaries, observing its functions, and selecting those parts which could be named and circulated in open rhetoric, people give shape to distinctive character of their cultural context. Collective identities in modern society take on specific bodily shapes, or are expressed in the aestheticization of that body's surface (Featherstone 1992).

As has been demonstrated at length by Michel Foucault (1977), the body is the surface on which messages of power are most clearly spelled out. It is also the arena in which political violence takes place and is given meaning and where resistance is articulated (Feldman 1991). Here conflicting interests are dramatized in the tension between the individual and collective search for identities.

What has to some extent been neglected in the cultural analysis of the body is its potential for producing the kind of truth that challenges social claims or already given definitions. It is frequently used as an entry into that secret domain to which the individual alone has the key, the private area to which he can return to find a definition of self unafflicted by societal restrictions or cultural categorization (Melucci 1991). Thereby it becomes the touchstone for questioning and reorganizing existing patterns.

Modernity has in a contradictory manner broadened the scope of collective identities and eagerly encouraged private experience; by the same token it has dispersed and deconstructed identities. As an outcome of this, the body has been allotted growing importance as the source of authenticity and continuity and as a zone of security in a constantly vicissious environment.

Within the course of this century, the interest people have paid to disciplining their own bodies and to investigating its possibilities is quite striking. We may perhaps, be able to view the full array of today's activities—from work-outs, jogging and aerobics to the obsession with skin, feelings and the sensual as a ritual where people try to seek out what is still unseen and unspoken. The body does not only produce security, but works also as an antenna to contemporary life. By keeping alert and through various channels people assimilate messages which are vaguely articulated and still not verbalized. Signals that are hard to apprehend are amplified and stored for further use. People primarily gain new experiences and investigate new identities physically before they begin to explore them cognitively (Jackson 1983).

Hence the attention paid to nature has been part of this activation and reorganization of the senses. Not only has the body been asked to produce an alternative and a more primordial truth, but it has been the connecting link to nature. The encounter with nature, represented an opportunity to get in contact with an open system, replenishing the many worn-out phrases given by modern superficiality. Everyone was free to take the healing waters of nature. The ritual union of body and nature then, could help people to discover their own ability. More frequently than ever nature has been used as the place for recreation, for repose as well as activity. Swedes are supposed to be nature-lovers. The important thing then is to see this, not as a tradition from peasant society, but as the logical outcome of a fast and thorough process of modernization.

We will here be focussing on the inter-war period. This was not exactly the era for a post-modern immersion in desires, lust or sensations. The bodily discourse was radical in contrast to the previous Victorian period, but it was more a question of domination than submission. Central concepts were: hardening oneself, endurance, daring, and self-discipline. This goes to prove that in this cleavage, the body became the instrument through which people tried to achieve certainty. When they subjected it to hardship, tested its strength, strove to toughen it and provoke pain, it was because they wanted to create a subject in a time of transformation— of dissolution as well as construction. Provoking pain—like the search for pleasure—was an attempt to achieve clarity on the frontiers of unclarity (Seremetakis 1991:4). In this phase of modernity the body became the training ground for the double process of educating the senses and making good use of them.

Modernization from Above

The period between the two world wars in Sweden was the official watershed for modernism in its functionalistic image. It became an export product reaching far beyond the narrow circles of the bourgeoisie, the intellectuals, and the general reading public. The tracks which were laid out at that time have since then dictated the course of the high-speed train called "The Swedish Model" (Frykman & Löfgren 1985).

Explanations for this have mostly invoked changes at the government level. At the start of the 1930s the Social Democrats began their four decades of unbroken power. They initiated reform policies to change not just the infrastructure of society but also the everyday lives of the citizens. Intellectuals who embraced functionalism's need-oriented, right-angled, and rational ideals rallied round the bastions of power, ready to stage the dreams that were now politically possible. Radical debaters like Gunnar and Alva Myrdal, Uno Åhrén, Greger Paulsson, Axel Höjer—to name just a few examples—were not in opposition to existing power structures; they were the social engineers whose ideas would be realized by the new rulers. Swedish intellectuals became reforming intellectuals during this era of transition (Eyerman 1991).

Among their ideas was included the faith that both social life and private life could be rationalized. Central and local authorities, architect's offices, school boards, and medical services were invaded by people who urgently wanted to improve the conditions for those worse off. Their goal was to introduce wise measures "to put life to rights" for the ordinary citizen (Hirdman 1989). "The Strong Society," as the Social Democratic prime minister Tage Erlander called the idea, was needed so that the weakest members could be helped.

Power over the Body

The citizens of the Swedish welfare state—"the home for the people"— were subjected to well-meaning attempts at colonization by people who knew how they should organize their day-to-day life and look after their bodies. The daily rhythm of the body, how long they should sleep and work, how many calories they needed, their dental status, mental hygiene, and sexual habits were scientifically defined and transformed into political issues. A broad area of contact was created between the rulers and the ruled.[4] The people in power sought to break down existing, backward habits and replace them with new, rational ones.

While the old bourgeois culture at the turn of the century was engaged in a civilizing project, where the body was shrouded in secrecy, and bodily functions were supposed to be concealed by taboo, the new attitude was one of liberation (See Frykman & Löfgren 1987). The rather pragmatic view held in pre-modern peasant culture was regarded as an example—left alone the ignorance and lack of discipline. The body ought to be part of the planned economy of the well-fare state, its functions, capacities and senses taken into use for the great leap forward.

When Sweden pioneered the teaching of sex education and sexual hygiene in schools, this was an example of the desire to rationalize the body and its drives—to make sensible use of them. Not only the church but also authorities and responsible citizens often expressed the fear that young people would be corrupted by "depraved" sexuality, which was a way of saying that irrationalism and prejudice ought to be uprooted. On the other hand, contact between the sexes should not be reduced to eroticism and lust—young boys and girls were supposed to understand the enormous potential for creating happiness, home and future that were within reach (Frykman 1988). Sexuality had to be made socially, economically and psychologically productive and beneficial. Various programs for enlightenment and education were launched; these tended to be exercises in hygienic behaviour more than introductions to a life of pleasures.

It has frequently been stated that the price which citizens had to pay for the state's considerateness was that they had to accustom themselves to the idea that someone else knew best (Arnstberg 1989). The strong society never needed to show its severity, just its wisdom. The rulers benevolently monitored the citizens.

In Foucault's terms we could point out the way Swedes internalized this control and made it their own: they became the subject, not the object, of the exercise of power. When Foucault says in *Discipline and Punish* (1977) that society showed its power by instilling in the senses of the citizens a will to become more efficient, orderly, and eager to look after their physical abilities, one wonders if he was thinking back to his stay in Uppsala at the end of the 1950s. Swedish power was not repressive but productive. Modernity, calling tradition to the stand and rationalizing the body was then part of change from above.

The Self-Understanding of the Middle Class

The picture of Sweden as the birthplace of conditional freedom can thus have a justified foothold in general consciousness. The state was a power factor with unparalleled influence. (There was also a long tradition of rule on which to build. For centuries the powers had been able to rely on a class of loyal officials who were obedient and ever-ready to serve.)

The 1930s also saw the breakthrough for the middle class, for the educated bourgeoisie, for the many experts. People spoke of the bright future when the aristocracy of intelligence would replace all previous nobility— the nobility that relied on violence, birth or wealth (Frykman 1987:192). Now the middle-class intellectuals spoke sympathetically about the people and the great working class; the majority of the population who were the numerically essential platform for the tribuneship to which the intellectuals were appointed. The crisis of legitimation which they would otherwise have faced when they approached power was solved by invoking their mandate from the people. They acted, not on the basis of their self-interest, but with the claim that their aims were higher and nobler (see Gouldner 1979).

The new civilizing middle class spoke the clear language of science and reason. The body, its functions and achievements were the focus for much of the reform work. The citizens of the welfare state had to be given a presentable form—molded after the ideal of the middle class. The importance of keeping clean, keeping fit, and rationalizing the domestic chores was not about the selling of an *ideology* or a moral program—this would have provoked an immediate reaction among the lower classes— but about spreading an ideology through *instruction in a method* (Frykman 1981, Frykman & Löfgren 1985). This was so much easier since the prudishness and double standard of the older bourgeoisie was seen as part of a deplorable and very premodern past.

But the translation from the reformative world's many ambitious programs to popular practice is always hazardous. Ethnological research in recent decades has shown the relative autonomy of the cultural organization of everyday life in relation to external influences. What could be seen as hegemonic processes from the centers of power, created opposition, variation and complexity when carried out. Welfare society created an official discourse of homogeneity and heterogeneity in practice.

One may indeed wonder whether the middle-class intellectuals of the 1930s were primarily preaching to each other. That which was truth in an artistic avant-garde or among far-sighted reformers remained a truth mostly for them alone. Suggestions which sought to rationalize everyday life surely got beyond the committee reports, the newspaper leaders, and the other educated arenas and reached the man in the street—in a very distorted way. The famous Stockholm exhibition in 1930,which marked the breakthrough of functionalistic architecture and home-decorating, produced dismay, fascination and opposition among ordinary people. They looked upon the flat roofs, shiny tubular steel furniture, and laboratory-like kitchens with amazement and horror. Only via after-the-fact historiography has the exhibition developed into something it never was in the culture of the times.

A flagrant example of this failure of the intellectuals to reach out beyond their own class is the nativity propaganda of the early 1940s. The population crisis of the 1930s was to be solved by encouraging families to have more children. In other words, they should rationalize their everyday lives in such a way as to see the favourable effects of sexuality's mental and emotional hygiene and to see large families as the path to happiness for themselves and society. The welfare of the individual and society were intertwined. The consequence of this intensive propaganda was naturally that priests, doctors, teachers, and other members of the middle class had many children. In the working class, by contrast, nativity fell to start with (Hatje 1974); they used the now permitted contraceptives to do the opposite of what the state wanted. The baby-boom of the 40s, was due to several other factors afflicting the West.

So, what has usually been seen as the start of the great leap towards societal reform was also part of a cultural formative process among hitherto vaguely coordinated members of a growing educated middle class. Where an earlier generation used capital and property as the foundation for their cultural formation, access to state policy and public opinion was now far more important.

This formation in itself was an important stage in the establishment of the middle class as reform-minded and progressive. They opened a path on which they would walk for a long time: they became more sensitive to demands from below. And they designed their cultural identity not so much in contrast to existing peasant or working-class patterns of the time, as with the physical demureness of the older generation as the Other. For the bourgeoisie at the turn of the century class-distinction was much more important, while their descendants brought in a more pronounced temporal dimension.

For the educated bourgeoisie, the reorganization of the senses was something that began in the word and then became flesh. For other social classes, immediate actions were of more sweeping importance.

The New Bodily Awareness

"If I were a dictator, I would forbid the playing of all ball games in England, making a possible exception for two days each week. Youths would do gymnastics according to the most rational Swedish system on the other days."

That was how the British minister Clark Kerr expressed himself for *Svenska Dagbladet* on 27 July 1934 just before his return home. The minister would not have survived for very long as a British dictator with such a program. A change of this kind cannot be imposed from above. Yet what he described as utopian for many Englishmen was a reality for many in Sweden. In just about every association's meeting-house, every community center, and every free gymnasium in the 1930s, people engaged in physical exercise. This was the same for young and old, for boys and girls, for workers, farmers, and bourgeois.

The Swedish Gymnastics Association, which at the end of World War I had scarcely 8,000 members, had by the beginning of the next world war expanded to more than 160,000 members. Only the organized members are counted here—not all physical fitness exercise was performed by registered gymnasts.

Without comparison, this was the fastest growing popular movement (in all categories) of the time. The expansion was not the result of an organizational triumph; on the contrary, it was borne aloft on a wave of born-again physical enthusiasm. It could certainly not be seen as the outcome of what was planned at the center. Governmental policy did certainly take up the same issues as were taken to the fore in these movements, but the interest paid to sport, gymnastics or outdoor activities from this part of society was truly insignificant.

Gymnastics must be understood in the light of the inter-war delight in *doing*, in *showing* and *talking about* what had previously been inconceivable or secret, in exploring the possibilities of a more mobile and swayed world. The word "gymnastics" then covered a wide range of activities. Some of them were carried out in gymnasiums or in outdoor arenas and ovals. But in the 30s, gymnastics also denotes an orientation towards a healthy regime for the body. As an expression of the spirit of the age and a yearning to change physical practice, and to discover new fields, gymnastics could be seen as one example (but an eloquent one) of the joy of discovery and the inquisitive will to experiment. Along with gymnasts we find keep-fit enthusiasts, vegetarians, scouts, nudists, and athletes.

The Body's Revolution

The new bodily awareness could be see in the dashing openness of relations between the sexes, of backslapping comradeship wherever like-minded people met. This was chiefly visible among young people, and it was they who indulged in the new patterns of movement, dancing to the modern tones and rhythms of jazz. A different sensuality and the sexual openness was also evident on the pages of contemporary books, on the silver screen, on the bandstands and the couches.

The Social Democratic journal *Morgonbris* in 1934 used dramatic adjectives to describe how politics almost failed to keep up with the rampant impatience of the body. Practice went before the formative discourse:

> It is a huge revolution. We are living in the middle of the body's revolution; we hardly notice it, but it is mightier than all political upheavals. It develops out of the same causes; the world must be remade, people's lives must assume other forms ... in order to endure one must have physical strength, a trained, well-formed body, flexible, well oiled—a machine to live with. This applies to the men. But it also applies to the women, who are violently wrenched out of an indolent existence in a fat corset and tight shoes. Make the body strong and shape it to be living, glad, and harmonious, and the soul will willingly follow in its tracks. The body's revolution is, therefore, more tremendous than all political upheavals (cited in Nilsson 1991:89).

The talk here is of a strategy of exploration, where one's own body was the first field to cover. What distinguishes the new body is impatience—the urge to leap forward. The impatience is directed both forwards and inwards: to try to reach the original sources. People have to reconquer both internal and external nature, to strengthen both body and soul. Like any important social and cultural movement, there is this concentration on the primary processes, a quest for authenticity where the body and the senses are regarded as the true basis for construction of a new identity (Melucci 1991). The body is defined as nature and placed outside of the instrumental rationality of "the world"—a world that must be re-made. It contains the deeply felt needs, needs and sentiments that have not been manipulated. In this new context the body is rediscovered.

Gymnastics was part of a thoroughgoing change which sought to stretch the body in a bold arc towards a future which could still only be imagined. The body had to be trained in order to be used. Still the body was to be transcended, a vehicle to be used to get somewhere.

Into the Open Air

The most suitable setting for the new body was the outdoors. All through the 1930s we find a longing to get away from civilization, away from the promises that had been broken with the First World War. Gymnastics was practiced in gymnasiums during part of the year, but this stuffy atmosphere was merely a makeshift solution, a preparation for the more authentic direct contact with the sources of authenticity.

One did not experience true life until one came out into the open, in the rays of the sun and the flowers of the meadow, with the forest or the ocean in sight. It was an outer and inner journey of discovery, but with a destination. To what hardships could one subject the body? How long could one lie in the water? How far could one cycle in a day? How did one feel to be bronzed after canoeing in the archipelago? The answers were still not clear. The surroundings channeled energy into the body. One also could hear the response in oneself.

When I wander here in the wilderness, I cannot help but reflect upon the fact that with each passing day I come ever more under nature's domination. For each passing day, I move with ever greater familiarity in the terrain; it is as if I increasingly come into correspondence with the objects, as if I were being sucked up by the environment, growing into and becoming a part of it. . . .

Is it not the case that this feeling makes itself felt more and more as your skin becomes hardened by the sun and wind? When you are still not suntanned, when you are still "city pale" and tender-skinned, as if you were afraid of nature, you feel lost and confused. But the more you are hardened, the more intimate you become with nature's different phenomena. It is a feeling which is invaluable. It is the entrance to the sanctuary of health.

It is precisely this union with nature which strengthens body and soul to such an undreamt-of degree. It is a peculiar thing, difficult to put into words. All of a sudden one feels like a part of the nature which one sees around one. The trees, the plants on the ground, the sea, the rays of sunlight which burn so pleasantly are no longer something external and alien, but something which belongs to my very essence, a part of myself. I am filled with something new which comes over me with a violent force, a feeling of fullness and harmony, of maturity and strength (Henzel 1934:82f).

This kind of popular vitalism could be easily traced in the innumerable photographs from annuals, magazines, and family albums, in which men and women pose against a background of cliffs, rivers, beaches and tents. The striking thing is that neither the individuals nor the arranged group are the main subjects. What is depicted is people as part of a landscape or natural scene. The smooth surface of the lake at the foot of the cliffs is complemented by the sight of the lad who is about to leap and break that surface. Life is given to the white birch trees and mossy stones in the pasture by someone standing on his hands and doing a back arch. Through movements bodies express nature; in movements bodies expropriate nature.

Nature is then not a Linnæan expert in the proper naming of flora and fauna, but an instructor in physical, training, and expression. For the bourgeoisie nature had been an object of study, full of species to be examined, named and arranged in hierarchies. Nature was producing otherness, that dangerous zone outside that must not become inside. The body should not be too closely associated with this disorderly but fascinating challenge to an orderly life (Featherstone 1992:286). Now it was turned into a cross-country track, an open-air gymnasium, a place for camping, something that could invigorate the body if properly used.

In order to give focus to this special interpretation of nature, one must keep in mind that this was not a sombre Teutonic romanticism where nature was dark, mystical and threatening as in the paintings of Caspar David Friedrich. Not something to conquer or transcend in fierce battle, but to utilize. Here we can find the bridging contact between a premodern (supposedly pragmatic) peasant culture and attitudes in welfare society. Now peasant society was serving as a model for how to relate to nature.

The landscape which people sought was hearty and healthy. There was here a disarming element of openness and liberation in people's poses and patterns of movement. Admittedly, there were also the athletic bodies of socialist realism or fascism, standing out at the expense of their surroundings. It seems more correct to say that a new bodily awareness was appropriated by different ideologies of the time.

It was not just gymnasts who set off on such voyages of discovery. And they were seldom ordered to use their holidays or leisure time to visit the beaches or walk in the mountains. This was the formative period of mass tourism, where the bicycle, the tent, the youth hostel and the canoe became the aids with which hundreds of thousands of people discovered Sweden. The programs for what people were supposed to experience came far behind what people actually did. In action people opened up new sensory registers, saw new horizons and by doing so constituted themselves into new identities. This by all means was part of a reflexive process where they could physically remove themselves from their everyday lives and shed new light on worn-out habits and traditions.

It was also characteristic that people acted as if nature were a part of the modern project. They did not just flee from the compulsions and pressures of society; they also sought the source of strength which they supposed nature to be. At the time when society's engineers were trying to ennoble the Swedish landscape with straight roads and precisely oriented power lines, the inhabitants were using it for the purposes of recreational activities. At the same time that modern attitudes were prescribed and new collective identities became possible, people were incited to and given the possibility of producing new individual identities.

Bodily Statements

In a very direct sense individual variation—together with discipline—was on display in this colonizing of nature and open spaces. What they did, was to go public with that which was most private.

If we stick to gymnastics and different fitness trainings, it is the absence of the élite or well trained athletic bodies that is most striking. It exists but does not rule. A single example could serve as an illustration.

One of the first journalists at the Swedish Broadcasting Corporation, Ingrid Samuelsson, has described the revelation she experienced one summer-afternoon in Stockholm: "Broadcasting was in its beginning, there was so much to explore and to do. As a reporter I was called upon to do a commentary on the *cooperative* House-wife Gymnastics, which was to be opened—or more correctly inaugurated—at an oval in the center of the city. I went there and before my eyes opened up an ocean of unbridled women, an ocean of abandoned corsets. Something new is happening, I thought, a new kind of women's liberation."

What these women were doing was nothing less than breaking the existing taboo on which bodies were allowed to be on public display. They were by no standards perfect, or normal in the disciplined sense: plain middle-aged women, thin and fat, newly married or worn out by children, were seen doing exercise on the green turf in the center of the city.

Quite ordinary bodies of both sexes were being exposed publicly, were being exercised over the radio and were shown in daily newspapers and magazines. It was a multitude of bodily presence hitherto never even dreamed of. Of course this capture, or seizure of public space was a matter of great moral concern and intense debate. A part of the very group that usually designs the image of the national—intellectuals and the educated middle class—was apalled. The exposure of so much bare skin was the sign of falling standards, moral decline and a cause of something close to moral panic.

This could not change the fact that the activity was a painstakingly visible statement about the variety of the bodies that were to be accepted as representing today's modern Sweden. Just by performing some of the rituals required by culture—here the gymnastic movements, or taking a swim or making a dash—the more or less naked body became in a way socially acknowledged.

There was another encouragement of complexity. What really happened when one went to a holiday-camp, joined the local gymnastical association or sports association was that new structures of communications were established. Bodies became able to imitate or quote bodies other than just those surrounding them in the family or local community. It was more than the obvious possibility of making friends and taking part in travels and games. In this kind of mimesis new restrictions were enforced at the same time that the possibilities opened for a multitude of new alternatives. New values were transmitted, and other sources of personal legitimation, and new belongings became possible.

The importance of these new bodily practices were evident. As people put their own bodies on public display, they introduced a considerable amount of discipline and restrain on those bodies; that was one side of the coin. On the other side, they also changed the public image.

In a Different Country

The view of country people was also redefined. National romanticism had been infatuated with genuine folk culture and its stout-hearted bearers, but this attitude was abandoned when people directed their gazes to the future. "One sneers at the traditional poetry of tourist albums, and the sight of a Dalecarlian woman dressed in the local costume provokes a sense of embarrassment" as someone wrote in the catalogue for the national leisure exhibition in Ystad in 1936.[5]

The countryside became a nationwide health institute. On purpose or in ignorance, people bypassed Skansen and the other open air museums which for a generation had been the shrines over the peasantry and national heritage. These did not represent a cultural heritage with which one could identify. The physical exercises people engaged in brought a different history to life. It was instead the farmer as a manual labourer who was taken to heart; the farmer who hardened his body and was weather-beaten, ate naturally cultivated crops, had a pragmatic and natural view of sexuality.

Leaving the cities and towns for the countryside was for many people a way to find the physical fitness program. Hundreds of thousands of youths partook in haymaking and harvesting, to experience the potential offered by working close to nature. Lodging a couple of weeks on a farm became an approved way of spending the holiday, reasonable in price and not at all ceremonious. This gave other perspectives than staying in a boarding house or following the usual bourgeois seasonal migration pattern between town and summer-house.

The physical occupation of the countryside produced other narrations and other experiences than the general discourse or written history. Contact with the past and the roots that were found in the countryside was founded upon action and hence less possible to include in already existing patterns.

The re-drawing of the picture of country life had some common features. People selected elements of life in the country and identified them as modern and rational. Here they identified practical directions in the art of living, hints which could then be used in everyday life in the office or the factory. Without either writing history or formulating utopias, people defined a lifestyle which excluded old patterns and adopted new ones. It was far more than a cultural program or an ideological construction. What we witness is not primarily a changed *view* or new narration. It was a changed *practice* which drove people into new spaces of experience. Through actions people gave the countryside a new content, at the same time as they changed their own bodily practice. This attitude, which in some respects was also typically modern, became a physical disposition and a skill, and later a new narrative about life in the countryside.

Paradoxically, rediscovering the countryside went hand in hand with the growing importance of city life. During the 30s, the lights from the streets and the many shop windows, the dreamworld of the flickers and the jazz-music from the dance halls and restaurants was ascribed an almost mystical attraction. The author Ivar Lo-Johansson portrays himself lying at night on a hill above his parents' cottage at quite some distance from Stockholm, looking at the lit-up clouds over the capital. The city was the place where authentic life was on display, day and night. Here you could be seen as the person you were meant to be, here you could explore new life styles and get in touch with other collective identities (Alsmark 1985).

The migration flow turned strongly to the urban areas during the period. But culturally, through mass media and especially the radio, city life and attitudes became present all over the nation. The old polarity between town and country were being redefined and in some areas considerably diminished. They both became arenas in which people could stay for a while, play the parts possible for them and move freely between the different parts. This transition was one of the very fundamentals for the reflexivity so immanent within the modern project. Experiencing complexity was the driving force for a further concentration on the shaping of the body.

The Simple Way of Life

Modern welfare society demanded—and opened the possibilities for—a more transparent bodily attitude. When people emphasized openness and health, this profiled the buttoned-up Victorianism in rather dark colours. People contrasted themselves against older patterns, thereby defining themselves in a temporal sequence, *on the move.*

The road to a better life was paved with all the promises of authenticity in the tiniest details of everyday life: wearing soft collars instead of the old chokers, comfortable shoes with plenty of room for the toes, and a practical and functional attitude towards leisure time; walking to work; doing physical labor; breathing fresh air; sleeping with a window open; eating healthy food; being daringly frank about matters which had previously been kept secret. All this was encapsulated in terms like simplicity and naturalness. It could all be combined with the modern project, with its willingness to break away and its desire to travel light, to bid farewell to the body closed up in a socially defined costume and instead find an outfit which permitted greater individual space and abandon.

The simple way of life was thus the start of the process of reorganizing—opening and reshaping—the senses. The body, with its habits and its external shell, became at once something malleable and something unknown.[6] People saw how they could create themselves through gymnastics and training; control their digestion and attain health through a correct diet; avoid illness by altering their lifestyle; build up their resistance by enduring hardship; discover their freedom by wearing loose-fitting track suits, shorts, and sandals. New arenas for action were opened, and new patterns of movement were created. Above all, people learned how to make the body open to new proposals, demands, and possibilities.

The Rationalization of Habits

This obsession with the physical can be discerned in various guises throughout Europe in the inter-war period, but nowhere was it as widely embraced by the people as in the Scandinavia countries and in Sweden. What made the situation here so unique?

The rationalizing of everyday habits and training for the great leap forwards were perhaps most earnestly advocated by the many different popular movements. The same modernist impatience was previously found in the free churches, the temperance movements, and the labour movement. Each had its own form of Utopia which transmuted today into a waiting-room for tomorrow.

When the legendary champion of temperance and popular movements, Justus Elgeskog, was requested in 1935, to comment on gymnastics, he poured words of praise over its intrinsic potential. "It could," he wrote, "place itself beside the other powers of health and make common cause with them in a conscious effort towards a way of life which was rational in all regards:"

> Gymnastics ... must expand to encompass all sides of modern life, which in association with gymnastics can become objects for enlightenment and education. Is it not rather strange that in a time when associations are being formed for just about everything, it is not considered necessary to create a special organization for *the promotion of a rational way of living.* Since no such organization exists ... its functions should be taken over by the Swedish Gymnastics Association (1935:289).

The goal of rationalizing one's way of life was an integral part of a better-known concept, with deeper roots than even the temperance movement. It was about the importance of living a reasonable and worthy life in which one did not become a slave under any enforced shackles, whether they took the form of alcohol, oppression from the powers that be, or deeply rooted habits of thought. Gymnastics was directly connected to the educational program which the popular movements had advocated for half a century. According to this, the individual personally bore the responsibility for his or her betterment. By carefully reading, reflecting, and acquiring long planning horizons, one could receive the inspiration to change one's own life. One must liberate oneself from the low animalistic and habitual impulses which prevented one from "stepping into the light". This attitude meant that people converted their own lives into a civilizing project in which every day was a struggle to raise oneself and achieve enlightenment. This in turn required that the individual had sufficient insight to free himself from whatever cultural context he happened to be enrolled in. The community to which people aspired was instead a future one, made up of other brothers and sisters sharing the same ideals.

It was not just nationalism which created an imagined community. In the labour movement, the temperance movement, and the free church the coin was intensively circulated and worn down by daily use.

This everyday rationalism, grounded in reading and studies, was not an invention of the nineteenth century's upward-moving popular movements. Instead, it had its roots in Lutheran pietism and in bible study. There existed the same direction of movement for the individual, namely to study the holy scriptures and through meditation attain knowledge about God's intentions (Ambjörnsson 1989). Arranging everyday life according to the new-found convictions was a part of life's sacrament. It meant reducing daily life to the absolutely most essential and giving up ostentatious display and folly.

This popular application of a more general Protestant ethic became the foundation for discipline *and* resistance. It gave moral support to challenging the ruling élites for their lack of virtue, to legitimizing alternative social patterns and preparing oneself for the advent of new social orders.

Consequently, when Justus Elgeskog pleaded for a rationalization of life, he struck a chord which was in harmony with Swedish popular movements and a widely embraced religious tradition. The music of gymnastics was remarkably familiar. Gymnastics promised to *do* what people had *preached* earlier. It was now time to move from words to action. One no longer needed to "satisfy oneself with *teaching* about rational ways of living; one must also *apply* it" (1935:290).

What now happened was that thought and speech were transformed into a physical program, which spoke about the importance of dreaming one's way into a future identity and stretching oneself beyond the existing daily conditions in order to attain something better. In this it exemplified the way modernization was accomplished from below and the change of the body was the logical continuation of something with roots reaching far back in history.

At the same time, the new body movements helped to reorganize the picture of the past. People found a continuity with a different, more down-to-earth, history than the idyllized version of the national romantics. Gymnastics and the rationalization of everyday life made Swedes more independent of the pompous official historiography. The much-discussed lack of history in Sweden would be hard to envisage without this form of bodily reorganization of the past.

The fact that the dreams had long been there, however, does not explain why they now were given shape in the 1930s. We must explore further.

Modernity and the Dynamics of Diversity

In the 1930s, we can observe an interesting interaction. At the same time that centrally initiated endeavors grow in their scope and intensity, people try to escape the disciplining efforts through counter-activities. Conversely, we can see how politics breathlessly tried to keep up with the ongoing revolution of the body, and tried to steer it into the desired channels. In physical exercise, sport, the health-food movement, mountain rambles, and the revolution of the senses, people sought out untried territories, alternative movements, new answers.[7] What people were looking for was not just new experiences but new truths. People's dreams of another life took on a concrete, attainable content. To become credible, the dreams had to be tested. The future was anticipated in a movement.

It is difficult to understand the dynamics of change in the 1930s if we do not see how the growing interest of the state fostered people's activity, how strategies of dominance were accompanied or preceded by attempts to conquer, and how the pace of change was speeded up in this struggle. The revolution of the body would have been unthinkable without the new welfare state's assiduous intervention in the citizens' physique. No matter how many reformers there were in positions of great influence, they would probably not have been able to change other people's everyday lives if this other factor had not arisen. The power to change did not just emanate from the government or one social group. On the contrary, Swedish modernity and propensity to change arose from thousands of encounters between people's everyday lives and the programs of the reformers. Indeed, it could be said that it was really here, on the periphery of imagined power, that the reform program was shaped, and it was in these encounters that the strong power of the state was defined and diversity produced.

The question, then, is not whether the middle class or the state actually succeeded in teaching the method—they did indeed, and highly effectively—but how it came about that the project was so successful and that the result was so multi-faceted. The change was possible because it was met by transforming processes from below. If cultural patterns, like power, grow out of everyday practice, it would be equally justified to turn the question upside down and ask whether it was the case that modernization was propelled as a popular counter-strategy. What we face, then, is a complex situation where a struggle is waged between different interests and where the actions have different goals. Cultural change was and remained extremely contradictory, and it is in the way this tension was expressed that the body typified its times.

The dramatic change of the 1930s thus becomes easier to grasp when it is seen in relation to the state's inquisitiveness about private life, to the emergence of new class constellations, and to the everyday attempts of people to investigate the possibilities of the new society through the body. No single factor outweighed the others; each was unthinkable without the interplay of the others. It was the complexity which was culturally organizing, a wealth of contrasts which gradually led to new constellations, new experiences, new dreams, new movements.

Writing and Making Modernity

We now have some answers to the question of how Sweden was transformed into a modern nation in such a short time, answers which are partially different from those found in conventional historiography. We must search where we are not used to finding, in everyday actions and the reorganization of the senses, as well as in the corridors of power. A disposition that was modern was already there as an aspiration with roots in pietism and popular movements. There was a ready mold into which the idea could be poured. The discourse that was created for the body was planted in unusually fertile soil. New instruments of power were also created; this made the change easier. No resistance was launched that was not at the same time part of a new accommodation; no reform was canvassed that was not at the same time codifying popular demands. In this new situation new identities are incessantly produced, more variation enforced. And it becomes totally unproductive to separate a central level from a local, the urban from the rural, the public from the private.

The primary feature in my analysis of the body's role in the process lies in the demonstration that the new age was not something which people primarily understood; it was something which they felt that they were actively conquering, testing, mastering. The new physical disposition did not merely symbolize the new age—it *was* it. Modernity was much more than a utopian or instrumental program, it was lived everyday experience.

This great transformation of the senses was tacit, non-discursive, so it was never integrated with historiography. The image of the Swedish twentieth century presented in textbooks and research includes the rationalizing radicals of the 1930s and the political blueprints for "the Swedish model". A narration is told about the transforming power of the reforms, of power emanating from the center. But where can we read about gymnastics, the sporting cabins, the canoeing and cycling holidays? Where are the many exercises in breaking away, without which the change would not have been possible? The books devote plenty of space to the people who thought that they controlled modernity, leaving no room for the people who actually *made* it. The corporal dexterity which they practiced belongs to an unwritten history.

Ambassador Clark Kerr's hope—in the unlikely event that he ever became dictator in England—of introducing the rational Swedish gymnastics program never got beyond the newspaper pages of *Svenska Dagbladet*. Swedish gymnastics was not just an athletics movement; it showed the experiences, dreams, and power structures that helped to modernize Sweden in the 1930's.

Notes

1. In fact the *discourse* on Swedishness is very close to what is said about people's attitudes in modernity (Berman 1982). It is then not so much a description of a national habitus, as it is a prescription of what it ought to be (Ehn, Frykman & Löfgren 1993).

2. Interactionist research into identity is about the rhetoric of boundaries and contrasts: how identity becomes negotiable in encounter situations. It is not by chance that research into ethnicity has had its self-evident theoretical platform. Clashes of culture force the difference to be made visible on the map, to use Bateson's words (1972). In an essay in the collective work *Nationella identiteter i Norden*, Anders Linde-Laursen (1991:16) discusses how Danishness has been defined through the years by contrast with the Swedishness which is more dominant in Scandinavia. For a hitherto less developed discussion on how a national bodily praxis or *habitus* is formed, see Bourdieu (1984).

3. This was the predominant perspective in the intellectual debate around civilizing processes in the 70's and 80's. How the state or centers of power did constitute a subject through different means of socializing the body and the senses was taken up by Michel Foucault (1977) and the German "Hannover School" (See Bezzel et al. 1974, Negt & Kluge 1981), developing some perspectives around body and the senses from the Frankfurt tradition.

4. Eugenics came as a consequence of the will to divide the population into different productive categories, where the "fittest" (who were usually members of the educated middle class) were encouraged to reproduce, while the least fit were dissuaded from it. At worst, the latter could be sterilized.

5. Quoted from Nilsson (1991:88). The author pithily points out that, "Hazelius' Dalecarlia lay far away from Ystad."

6. The scholarly discussion which now received growing legitimacy was about psychology interpreted not in genetic but in physical terms. What could one learn of a person's character and ability from his body posture and musculature? What links were there between external form and inner qualities? Theories about the attributes that went along with different statures (athletic, leptosome, pyknic, etc.) gained wide acceptance among intellectuals.

7. This also created the passive strategies of escape, with a common form of popular protest being symbolized by idling on a sofa. The cartoon figure Kronblom made his appearance as the irrational resistance fighter, with laziness as his chief weapon (see Löfgren 1991).

References

Alsmark, Gunnar. 1985. Ljus över bygden. In: Frykman, Jonas & Löfgren, Orvar (eds): *Modärna tider*. Malmö: Liber.

Ambjörnsson, Ronny. 1989. *Den skötsamme arbetaren*. Stockholm: Carlssons.

Anderson, Benedict. 1983. *Imagined Communities. Reflections on the Origin and Spread of Nationalism*. London: Verso.

Arnstberg, Karl-Olov. 1989. Svenskhet. *Den kulturförnekande kulturen*. Stockholm: Carlssons.

Bateson, Gregory. 1972. *Steps to an Ecology of Mind*. New York: Ballantine Books.
Berman, Marshall. 1982. *All that is Solid Melts into Air: The Experience of Modernity*. New York: Simon & Shuster.
Bezzel, Chris et al. 1974. *Das Unvermögen der Realität*. Berlin.
Bourdieu, Pierre. 1984. *Distinction: A Social Critique of the Judgement of Taste*. Cambridge: Harvard University Press.
Daun, Åke. 1989. *Svensk mentalitet. Ett jämförande perspektiv*. Stockholm: Tiden.
Dumont, Louis. 1986. *Essays on Individualism. Modern Ideology in Anthropological Perspective*. Chicago: University of Chicago Press.
Ehn, Billy, Jonas Frykman & Orvar Löfgren. 1993. *Försvenskningen av Sverige*. Stockholm: Natur och Kultur.
Elgeskog, Justus. 1935. Rationell livsföring—ett problem för dagen. *Riksföreningen för gymnastikens främjande, Årsbok*.
Eyerman, Ron. 1991. De intellektuella och staten: en analytisk modell med speciell hänvisning till USA och Sverige. *VEST—Tidskrift för vetenskapsstudier*, 1.
Featherstone, Mike. 1992. Post-Modernism and the Aestheticization of Everyday Life. In: Lash, Scott & Friedman, Jonathan(eds): *Modernity and Identity*. Oxford: Basil Blackwell.
Feldman, Allen. 1991. *Formations of Violence. The Narrative of the Body and Political Terror in Northern Ireland*. Chicago: University of Chicago Press.
Foucault, Michel. 1977. *Discipline and Punish. The Birth of the Prison*. Harmondsworth: Allen Lane.
Foucault, Michel. 1980. *The History of Sexuality*, Vol. 1. New York: Pantheon.
Frykman, Jonas. 1981. Pure and Rational: The Hygienic Vision. *Ethnologia Scandinavica*.
Frykman, Jonas. 1987. The Educating Class. In: *Kinderkultur* 25, Deutscher Volkskundekongress. Bremen: Hefte der Focke-Museums.
Frykman, Jonas. 1991. Modernitet som svensk mentalitet. In Agrell, Wilhelm (ed): *Nationell säkerhet utan gränser* Stockholm: Allmänna Förlaget.
Frykman, Jonas & Orvar Löfgren. 1987. *Culture Builders. An Historical Anthropology of Middle Class Life*. New Brunswick: Rutgers University Press.
Frykman, Jonas & Orvar Löfgren (eds.). 1985. *Modärna tider. Vision och vardag i folkhemmet*. Malmö: Liber.
Frykman, Jonas & Orvar Löfgren (eds.). 1991. *Svenska vanor och ovanor*. Stockholm: Natur och Kultur.
Gouldner, Alvin. 1979. *The Future of Intellectuals and the Rise of the New Class*. New York: Oxford University Press.
Hatje, Ann-Katrin. 1974. *Befolkningsfrågan och välfärden. Debatten om familjepolitik och nativitetsökning under 30- och 40-talen*. Stockholm: Allmänna Förlaget.
Henzel, Roland. 1934. *Årsbröder emellan*. Stockholm: Natur och Kultur.
Hirdman, Yvonne. 1989. *Att lägga livet till rätta. Studier i svensk folkhemspolitik*. Stockholm: Allmänna Förlaget.
Jackson, Michael. 1983. Knowledge of the Body. *Man* 18.
Lash, Scott & Jonathan Friedman (eds.). 1992. *Modernity and Identity*. Oxford: Basil Blackwell.

Linde-Laursen, Anders. 1991. ". . . derfra min verden går"—om nationell ident-
itet. In Linde-Laursen, A & Nilsson J-O: *Nationella identiteter i Norden—ett fullbordat projekt?* Eskilstuna: Nordiska Rådet.

Lindqvist, Mats. 1988. Var dag den andra lik? *Häften för kritiska studier* 3.

Löfgren, Orvar. 1984. Våra vänner i naturen. In Ambjörnsson Ronny & Gaunt,
David (eds): *Den dolda historien*. Stockholm: Författarförlaget.

Löfgren, Orvar. 1991. Nationalizing Modernity. *Paper presented at the seminar
Comparative Modernities.* Lund. Mimeo.

Marcus, George. 1992. Past Present and Emerging Identities. Requirements
for Ethnographies of Late Twentieth-Century Modernity Worldwide. In:
Lash, Scott & Friedman, Jonathan(eds): *Modernity and Identity*. Oxford: Basil
Blackwell.

Melucci, Alberto. 1991. *Nomader i nuet. Sociala rörelser och individuella behov i
dagens samhälle.* Göteborg: Daidalos. Transl.1989: *Nomads of the Present: Social
Movements and Individual Needs in Contemporary Society.* London.

Negt, Oskar & Kluge, Alexander. 1981. *Geschichte und Eigensinn.* Frankfurt am
Main.

Nilsson, Jan-Olof. 1991. Modernt, alltför modernt. Speglingar. In Linde-Laursen,
A & Nilsson, J-O (eds): *Nationella identiteter i Norden—ett fullbordat projekt?*
Nordiska Rådet.

Seremetakis, C. Nadia. 1991. *The Last Word. Women, Death and Divination in Inner
Mani.* Chicago: University of Chicago Press.

Weber, Eugen. 1977. *Peasants into Frenchmen. The Modernization of Rural France
1870–1914.* Stanford: Stanford University Press.

Åström Lissie. 1985. Husmodern möter folkhemmet. In Frykman, Jonas &
Löfgren Orvar (eds): *Modärna tider. Vision och vardag i folkhemmet.* Malmö:
Liber.

6

From Desert Storm to
Rodney King via ex-Yugoslavia:
On Cultural Anaesthesia

Allen Feldman

"We lost any sense of seasons of the year, and we lost any sense of the future. I don't know when the spring was finished and I don't know when the summer started. There are only two seasons now. There is a war season, and somewhere in the world there is a peace season."[1]

—Resident of besieged Sarajevo

In March 1992, I spoke, by invitation, at a conference titled *Violence and Civilizational Process* which was held in Sweden, where I had been teaching. My topic was violence and everyday life in Northern Ireland (see Feldman 1991a). A Croatian folklorist, the other foreign guest, talked on the culture of fear in the former Yugoslavia.[2] The rest of the presentations concerned the rationalization of violence by the state in the process of Swedish nation building. The conference theme was inspired by the work of Nobert Elias (1982), who had argued that modernization entails the progressive withdrawal of violence from everyday life in tandem with its increasing monopolization by the state. This stratification may have been felicitous coloring for 'mainstream' European modernization, but could only be dismissed as a bureaucratic conceit when considering the current situations of Northern Ireland and the former Yugoslavia. In these locales the state, in various ethnic and legal incarnations, has pursued hegemony by democratizing violence through the clandestine support of populist paramilitary terror.[3] In Northern Ireland and the various ethnic enclaves of Bosnia, Croatia and Serbia, the state's capacity to flood everyday life with violence has been enabled by the sequestering of political aggression behind legal, procedural and nationalist facades. This potent combination of instrumental rationality, state formalism and public terror can not easily be explained by the evolutionary drive of Norbert Elias's notion of civilizational process.

Due to their adherence to Elias's perspective, and their own biographical experience in Sweden, the local ethnologists and historians attending the meeting had difficulty conceptualizing political violence as a routinized element of everyday life; a concept without which it is impossible to grasp what has been happening in Northern Ireland for the last two decades, and more recently in ex-Yugoslavia. In discussion it became clear that for most of the scholars violence, like the geographies it had disordered, occupied the verges of civilizational process and European modernity. Violence linked to, and defining of, the cultural Other confirmed the exceptionalism of the historical and geographical periphery.

This tacit ghettoization was momentarily shaken as the Croatian folklorist delivered a paper punctuated, in the white space between her words, by barely concealed emotional disorder approaching public mourning. This was not her after-shock from living in a war zone, nor the catharsis of having momentarily exited. Rather her distress exposed the frustration, risk and uncertainty of communicating local terror to an audience at a historical and experiential remove. I was thrown back to the enforced spaces of silent fear I had encountered, doing fieldwork in Belfast, among those who were intimate with the regularity of random violence and who could not trust me with this intimacy of which, at that time, I had no bodily experience. How does one transport the experience of everyday terror that is almost inexpressable outside the sensory encompassment of violence? The Croatian did not speak explicitly of the sensory alterity she had made tangible in that conference room, rather it was borne by her body and voice. Incarnate sensory difference was the gulf where explicit theoretical communication hesitated. The Croatian's tension was about speaking, without guarantee of perceptual connection, to an audience who inhaled different cultural givens, touched different material realities, and who did not have to sniff out imminent death from once familiar surrounds.[4]

The Croatian was in search of a translatable language of terror, the conversion of local dread into mobile cultural form. She spoke of "ethnographic self-reflexivity," a concept glossed from recent criticism in American anthropology. But in contrast to the mentalist, confessional and text-centered tendencies of this approach, what emerged from her presentation was a palpable and gendered[5] self-reflexivity that had been channeled by the sensory remembrance of scheduled terror.

The grief in her voice and body rewrote her text as she spoke it, and opened up a historical and experiential chasm that no one could easily cross, but could at least acknowledge. Recognition of cultural difference was not forthcoming. Rather, the terms of dialogue were set immediately after she had finished speaking-mourning, as her first interlocuters rushed to insulate the room from the vortex of history-as-pain and to smooth the now broken plane of cultural presupposition. They fired defusing questions about media imagery, newspaper reportage and the like; subjects as reassuringly global as unvoiced sensory terror were deemed site specific. The audience moved from unease to animation as the discussion gravitated to the issue of how the Serbian and Croatian media were diversely depicting the war, though they had just witnessed the Croatian choking on the experiential inadequacy of conventional representation. Confronted with the personification of intractable materialities, authoritative questioners forcefully rerouted the conference to familiar culture-bound platforms from which to address the question of violence. This thematic shift may have been sheer politeness in the face of bared emotions, but I could not help but experience it as culturally mediated misdirection. The talismanic invocation of media imagery and issues provided a reassuring social narrative (certainly not limited to Swedes or scholars) on which to hang *cultural anaesthesia:* the banishment of disconcerting, discordant and anarchic sensory presences and agents that undermine the normalizing and often silent premises of everyday life. The segue into media practice and form and the avoidance of the speaker's situated sensibility, replicated the very effects of the first world's media processing of "exotic" violence; in this context the media was simultaneously critiqued and fetishized by the discussants.

The audience's response thereby encapsulated Elias's theory as cultural symptom: violence was withdrawn from the everyday and its disturbing perceptual dispositions were confined and silenced by invoking the informational norms of a universalizing rationality. It made no difference that the questions were after truth through the documentation of the media's distortion of "objectivity," for the general discussion presupposed, to the detriment of exposed embodied fear, that media criticism was a more suitable forum for grasping historical events. The audience's easy identification with media imagery, to which we are all susceptible, symbolically rescued the subject of violence from the alien sensorium evoked by the Croatian, and delivered it to an ethnocentric apparatus of historical perception.

All of this inadvertently demonstrated the extent to which violence and its consequences are automatically associated with aberrant cultural difference, and then tamed by exclusions that enable the self-serving perceptual negotiation of that difference. My own unvoiced questions were directed to the total dynamic symbolized by the conference dialogue, in which I was also culturally implicated: How does the *periphery* speak truth to the *center* if the very construct center/periphery is conditioned by the inadmissibility of alien sensory experience? When the Other is caught in, and even identifies with the powerful and mirroring gaze of direct or indirect mass media culture, what other perceptual options have been banished, closed and delegitimized by cultural anaesthesia?

*   *   *

Cultural anaesthesia is my gloss of Adorno's (1973) insight that in a post-Holocaust and late capitalist modernity the quantitative and qualitative increase of objectification increases the social capacity to inflict pain upon the Other[6]—and I would add—to render the Other's pain inadmissible to public discourse and culture.[7] It is upon this insight that a political anthropology of the senses in modernity can be elaborated. This formula implies that the communicative and semantic legitimacy of sensory capacities, and their ability to achieve collective representation in public culture, is unevenly distributed within systems of economic, racial, ethnic, gender, sexual and cultural domination.[8] Adorno's point about modernity's pain can be linked to the respective theses of Lukács (1971), Foucault (1978), Jameson (1981) and Corbin (1986) that the construction of the modern political subject entailed the stratification and specialization of the senses, and the consequent repression of manifold perceptual dispositions.[9] As a driving force in this historical dynamic, the mass media's depiction of the agents and objects of violence is crucial to the modernizing embodiment of those political subjects who occupy both sides of the screen of public representation. This is all the more pertinent when the very embodied character of violence is evaded, ignored or rewritten for collective reception.

Like other institutions (industrial, penological, psychiatric, and medical) the mass production of facts, *and of facticity itself,* are based on techniques and disciplines that, in the case of the media, materially mold a subject and culture of perception. The mass media has universalizing capacities that promote and inculcate sensory specializations and hierarchical rankings such as the priority of visual realism and the often commented on gendered or racial gaze. Like the normative optics of gender and race, objective realism, the depictive grammar of the mass media, should not be perceived as an ahistorical given; it is an apparatus of internal and external perceptual colonization that disseminates and legitimizes particular sensorial dispositions over others within and beyond our public culture.

In the 19th century, "realism" was associated with modes of narration and visualization that presumed an omniscient observer detached from and external to the scenography being presented. It was linked to formal pictorial perspectivism, and narrative linearity with all its assumptions about causality, space and time. Yet during this period cultural and scientific attention gradually detached itself from exclusive concentration on the scene observed and also focused on dissecting and representing the act of observation itself (Crary 1991). The perceiving subject could no longer remain external once perception became one object among others of realist representation. The scientific objectification of perception dovetailed with the latter's commodification by such forces as new media technologies, the manufacture and consumption of reproducible mass articles and experiences, advertising, new leisure practices, the acceleration of time and the implosions of urban space; all of which involved the remolding of everyday sensory orientations.

Ernst Bloch (1990), in the 1930s, redefined"realism" as *the cult of the immediately ascertainable fact* thereby pointedly linking it to norms of rapid and easy consumer satisfaction. More recently, David Harvey's (1989) spatial analyses implicitly point to the historical connection between the mass production/consumption of facticity and the apparent increase in perceptual mobility that accompanies the space/time compression characteristic of late modernity. Space/time compression can be defined as the implosion of perceptual simultaneity—the sudden abutment of persons, things, and events from a plurality of locales and chronologies and levels of experience once discrete and separate. Harvey attributes this, not only to technological advances, but to the accelerated circulation and efficient distribution of commodities, and to the permeation of exchange values in which new objects, spaces and activities become commodifiable and measurable and thus interchangeable with each other. When previously uncommodified things, activities and spaces become interchangeable and substitutable, and carry mobile valuations, they take on new temporal and spatial coordinates for human perception (Feldman 1991b).

The economic and psychic binding of perceptual practice to consumer satisfaction, discernment and skills generates a pseudo-mastery over "the real" through the experience and manipulation of simultaneity. The media's mass production and commodification of visual and audio facticity both creates and depends upon a perceptual apparatus of holistic realism. Here the ingestion of totality, perceptual holism, the personal capacity to encompass things through prosthetics becomes a valued commodity in itself. The holistic apparatus frequently jettisons the indigestible depth experience of particular sensory alterities. This is the case when sensory difference conflicts with the myth of immediate and totalizing perceptual command by resisting norms of accelerated consumption and the easy disposability of things (Seremetakis 1991b). These complex interactions of perception, space, time, facticity, events and material culture pose an eminently modernist dilemma: *that the perception of history is irrevocably tied to the history of sensory perception.*[10]

*   *   *

Cultural anaesthesia is a reflexive passageway into historical consciousness and representation, as Alain Corbin (1986) pointed out when he complained that western history, as written, has no odor. In the mass media cultural anaesthesia takes many forms. Generalities of bodies, dead, wounded, starving, diseased and homeless are pressed against the television screen as mass articles. In their pervasive depersonalization, this anonymous corporeality functions as an allegory of the elephantine "archaic" and violent histories of external and internal subalterns. The panopticism of documentary television, like its penological predecessor (Foucault 1978)[11], creates a new cellular intervention that captures and confines disordered and disordering categories of bodies. Staged, mounted, framed and flattened by a distilling electronic sieve, these icons of the static become moral inversions of the progressively malleable bodies of the ideal American viewer; the latter's public body is sensualized and mythicized by the orchestration of commercial messages on cosmetics, exercise, automobiles, fashion, dieting, recreation and travel. This visual polarity between the reformable bodies of the observer and the determined, deformed and reduced bodies of the observed, disseminates for the viewing public, a cultural scenario first associated with Hegel's master/slave dialectic: that relations of domination are spatially marked by the increase of perceptual (and thus social) distance from the body of the Other that is essentialized by material constraints that deny it recognizable sentience and historical possibility (Kojéve 1969).[12]

But cultural anaesthesia can also disembody subjects, which is what occurred in crucial segments of the televising of Operation Desert Storm. Here the media both pre-empted and then merged with the American military arsenal through the video erasure of "Arab" bodies. In order to fuse perceptual dominance with topographic conquest enemy bodies were electronically "disappeared" like the trouble makers in Joseph Heller's novel *Catch 22* (1961); Iraqi's were magically transmuted into infinitesimal grains of sand that threatened American war machinery. Here the body vanished was a priori the body vanquished. And a mass war against the built environment was mystified as a crusade against the desert as Orientalist topography.

The eulogized smartbombs were prosthetic devices that extended our participant observation in the video occlusion of absented Iraqi bodies. What were these celebrated mechanisms but air-borne televisions, visualizing automatons, that were hurled down upon the enemy creating his conditions of (non)visibility. Their broadcast images functioned as electronic simulacra that were injected into the collective nervous system of the audience as antibodies that inured the viewer from realizing the human-material consequence of the war. Visual mastery of the campaign pushed all other sensory dimensions outside the perceptual terms of reference. Culturally biased narrations abetted by informational technology historically molded to normative concepts of sensory truth precluded any scream of pain, any stench of corpse from visiting the American living room.

The spectatorship cultivated by the televising of Desert Storm cannot be reduced to voyeurism as some have suggested (see Stam 1991). For perceptual entanglement with the video simulation of the war was crucial to the manufacturing of consent, and thus politically and instrumentally implicated the viewing public in the action of violence. For even when a voyeur acts through a surrogate, it is to avoid material complicity not to share in it. Yet in Desert Storm the perceptual tools of the media exploited and elaborated the post-Vietnam political fantasy of American re-empowerment. This meta-narrative blurred the effective and moral distance between viewing and acting. Here sensory selection was a productive apparatus fashioning mutual political agency (and not passivity) between those who acted by looking and those whose acts of death were cinematized. Civilian television observation was continuous with the military optics of the fighter pilot and bombardier who were dependent on analogous prosthetic technology, and who killed at a distance with the sensory impunity and omniscient vision of the living room spectator. The combat crews who played with aggressive drives by watching pornographic videos prior to flying missions, demonstrated the uniform sensorium between viewing and violence as they up-shifted from one virtual reality to another.

*   *   *

It didn't make any sense to me, I couldn't see why they were doing what they were doing . . . He moved, they hit him . . . I was trying to look at and view what they were looking at . . . Evidently they saw something I didn't see. (Los Angeles Police Department Officer Theodore Brisenio on the arrest of Rodney Glen King)[13]

Less than two months into Operation Desert Storm the effaced body of the Other reappeared close at hand with the televised beating of Rodney King. Originally visualized outside the prescribed circuits of fact production, this black body broke through the nets of anaesthesia. Its shock effect derived not only from long-standing racial scars, but from the concurrent myth being played out with Desert Storm. The media campaign in the desert succeeded in cleansing post-Vietnam state violence. But the images of King's beating showed the state making pain. Here unprogrammed sensory substitution took place. Even the viewer insulated by race and class could experience the involuntary projection of his/her body to that point of the trajectory marked by the swinging police batons as they came down upon the collective retina which was suddenly rendered tactile. The spectacle of state manufactured trauma interdicted the visual myth of sanitary violence. King's beating was the skeletal X-ray image flashed upon the technologized surface of state rationality. Desert Storm and the beating of Rodney King evolved into two irreconcilable national narratives. Desert Storm celebrated a triumphalist sense of an ending, while King's beating laid bare another layer of wounding encounters: unfinished history as mise-en-scène—bound to return in the near future despite all attempts to change channels.[14] Two antagonistic icons of national experience impinged on the public screen of electronic consciousness without resolution, without one set of images offering a coherent account for the other.

It is no coincidence that a year later the dominant tropes of Operation Desert Storm seemed to work their way into the juridical reconstruction of King's beating. The trial of the Los Angeles police officers rescripted King's video. This reconstruction successfully returned the violence inflicted upon King to the protective corridors of state rationality. The legal restitution of state violence drew upon the depth structures of neo-colonial racial logic that had worked so well in the Desert Storm propaganda: the qualification of the body of the Other by geography; disembodiment of the Other's pain; the facilitation of cultural anaesthesia for all those who could be rendered directly or indirectly accountable for the pain of the Other.

The actual beating of Rodney King and its subsequent jural reconstruction mobilized a series of spaces within which King's body could be processed as a racial, a disciplinary, and a legal object. Through this metonymy of spaces, explicit and inferred, King achieved a dynamic visibility within which the video of beating was only a trailer.

Twenty minutes prior to the King's car being stopped by the police, Officer Powell taped that infamous statement into his communication unit concerning a recent case: "Sounds almost as exciting as our last call, it was right out of *Gorillas in the Mist*" (Courtroom Television Network: 1992). He was referring to a domestic quarrel involving an African-American family, though he later denied any racial connotation to the remark. In gravitating to this image, the media and the prosecution missed its deeper significance by artificially detaching its racist imagery from the everyday exercise of state power. Beyond and below state formalism, legal codes and official police procedures, there lies a symbolic logic of the state, animated by empowering micro-practices of depersonalization, that is readily fed by and articulated with culturally in-place racist archetypes.

The phrase "gorillas in the mist" in this instance, clearly evokes the jungle, the wilderness, the frontier; outside spaces opposed to a civilizational interior. These are pre-social naturalized terrain from which the sanctioned enforcer extracts the disciplinary subject as so-much "raw material" to be reworked by the state.[15] Likewise, the mythic anti-societal zones from which the disciplinary subject is obtained, mark the latter's embodiment as pre-social through the stigma of animality. The bodily alterity of the suspect-as-animal predetermines the material character and physical locus of police action on their captive. Bestial imagery continued to leak into subsequent characterizations of King made by defense witnesses and the accused. King was referred to as "bear-like" (Riley 1992a), and as "getting on his haunches" by Officer Powell in testimony. (Courtroom Television Network 1992).[16]

Animal imagery may have informed Officer Powell's project of both taming and caging King within a prescribed spatial perimeter, a practice that has both penal and racial overtones. He made the following statements during his examination by his attorneys and the prosecution:

> I yelled at him (King) to get down on the ground, to lay down on the ground ... he repeated the motion again, getting up again ... I stopped and evaluated whether he was going to lie there on the ground or whether he was going to get up again ... It was a continuing series of him getting back up on his arms, pushing up, sometimes raising to his knees, sometimes getting on his haunches. I commanded him to get down on the ground and when he wouldn't go for it, I hit him in the arms and tried to knock him back down.

At one point the prosecutor asked: "What was the reason for hitting him?" Powell replied:

> "I didn't want him to get back up."
> "What were you striking at?"
> "I was striking at his arms ... I was trying to knock him down from the push up position, back down onto the ground where he would be in a safer position ... I was scared because he was being told to lie down on the ground; he was getting hit with the baton several times and he continued to get back up ... I was looking up for something else to keep him down on the ground." (Courtroom Television Network: 1992)

It took Officer Powell 46 blows with his baton to incarcerate King into the spatial corridor he called "the ground." Officer Powell's geographical perception moved from "jungle" to "the ground," a provisional and surrogate territory of the state, while King, through violence, was shifted from animality to a subject in compliance. Sergeant Charles Duke, the defense's police procedures expert, described this compliance as viewed from the video.

> ...when he was in a flat position, where his feet were not cocked, where they were straight up and down and where his hands were above his head or at his side, he was not hit." (Courtroom Television Network 1992)

Sergeant Stacey Koon, the presiding officer at the scene of King's beating, also testified to the meaning of this posture and added that at this point King's bodily response and directed speech to the officers beating him signaled the final level of compliance. The successful confinement of King—the symmetry of a body lying at attention with the face in the dirt—*and* the acquisition of linguistic reciprocity marked the neutering of the animalized body and its internalization of the will of the state. A "gorilla-in-the mist," a black "bear" that insisted on rising on its "haunches" was turned by violence into a speaking subject. Official LAPD procedures underwrite this civilizing sequence. Police department directives on the use of violence while performing an arrest locate the subject capable of discourse at the lowest end of the scale of non-compliance and physical intervention. The subject in *logos* is the subject in law. The further removed the arrestee is from language, the closer the suspect is to the body and thus closer to escalating violence by the state. It is my suggestion that for the police who beat him, this violent passage of King from animality and the body to language and compliance intimately involved judgments concerning his capacity to sense and to remember pain.

Rodney King had to be taken to a hospital after his beating. Medical attendants assisting at his treatment testified to the following statements made by Officer Powell (and denied by him) to King, who worked at a sports stadium: "We played a little hardball tonight. Do you *remember* [emphasis added] who was playing? ... we won and you lost." (Riley 1992a:30)

It is a moment of reflection and summation after the act. King's wounds are being tended at the instruction of the man who beat him. The author of violence, grown intimate after his labors, inquires after his prisoner if he can recollect what has passed between them, and whether he recognizes the social relation they have entered. This inquiry presumes King's participation in common cultural ground; a mutuality that exists for Officer Powell only after the violence. Baseball, as a ludic metaphor of male dominance, converts batons into bats. King's recognition of this conversion, the admission of a shared culture of sport, more than being another stage in his socialization, would normalize the violence inflicted on him thus placing Powell's acts within the realm of the acceptable.

It is through this dialogue of recognition that the agent of violence re-trieves what he has authored through his acts. What is expected to answer him is his creation, his violence and his body doubled by the logos and submission of the subaltern. Powell's hospital discourse is too deeply anchored in the narratology of torture to have been fabricated. Artifice follows political life here. In *The Day of the Scorpion*, the second volume of Paul Scott's *Raj Quartet* (1978), an analogous encounter takes place between a white English policeman and his Indian prisoner he has just finished beating. The victim, Hari Kumar, describes "the situation"—the creation and acknowledgment of dominance through torture—to an ex-post facto government investigation:

> "What in fact was this situation? . . ."
> "It was a situation of enactment."
> "These ideas of what you call the situation were the DSP's (District Su-perintendent of Police) not your own?"
> "Yes he wanted them to be clear to me . . . Otherwise the enactment would be incomplete . . . The ideas without the enactment lose their signif-icance. He said if people would enact a situation they would understand its significance . . . He said that up until then our relationship had only been symbolic. It had to become real . . . He said . . . (it) wasn't enough to say he was English and I was Indian, that he was ruler and I was one of the ruled. We had to find out what it meant . . . the contempt on his side and the fear on mine . . . He said . . . we had to enact the situation as it really was, and in a way that would mean neither of us ever *forgetting*" [empha-sis added]. (Scott, 1978: 298–99)

In his own "situation of enactment" Powell confirms the socializing function of his graphic usage of King's body. Through violence King, like Hari Kumar, is meant to acquire *memory*, a history of who "won" and who "lost." King is asked to recollect hierarchy, its origin and his position in it. He has been progressively shifted from the jungle to the liminality of his beating ground only to come home to a baseball diamond, a preem-inent terrain of American normalization (where he was subjected to hardball or became one). These qualifying spaces, jungle, ground, base-ball field, and their various personae, gorillas, bear and hardball trace the incremental objectification of King and the gradated effacement of his subjecthood *and his pain*. King's pain achieves presence, only at the end of this progression and solely as an artifact of power; it is the affective pres-ence of the state within his body and person. This is why Officer Powell speaks to King about baseball, memory and hierarchy at precisely the moment that his victim is receiving medical attention. Police violence assaulted King's body, police ordered medical treatment attempts to re-dress the effaced sensory integrity of that body, thereby crediting the now socialized King with somatic capacities denied to him during the beating (see below). It is at this juncture that Powell asks King to remember through the senses, through the vehicle of recalled pain. Removal and manipulative restoration of the senses facilitates the state's coercive construction of personal memory and identity (see Feldman 1991: 128–38). Hari Kumar, in Scott's novel, identifies the attempted restitution of sensory integrity by his aggressor as the last act of political degradation ". . . the offer of charity, he gave me water. He bathed the lacerations" (Scott 1978: 299)

* * *

The final territorialization of King's body took place at court. Isolated frames of the video were time-coded by the prosecution, and freeze-framed and grid-mapped by the defense as if the event was an archaeological site. This reorganization of the video's surface resembled the video grids superimposed upon their targets by the smart bombs of Desert Storm. In the Simi Valley courtroom, fragments of action and isolated body parts achieved visibility as material evidence through this type of segmentation. The grid mapping detached King's limbs from each other in a division of labor which sorted out pertinent parts and actions from inadmissible and irrelevant residues. Visual dissection of King's body provided the defense argument with crucial perceptual fictions that were culturally mediated as objective and real. Thus cinematized time informed the following analysis of King's videoed postures by Sergeant Duke, the defense's police procedures expert: "It would be a perception that position 336:06 [time code] to be an aggressive position" (Courtroom Television Network, 1992). This discourse was possible because of the colonization of King's body by the virtual temporalities of slow motion, fast forward and freeze frame. With cinematic artifice, King's body was montaged into a purely electronic entity with no inwardness or tangibility. His body became a surface susceptible to endless re-editing and rearrangement as it suited both the prosecution and the defense. Further by automatically admitting such cinematic fictions and grammars as *material evidence* and as objective data, the court collapsed the perceptual and temporal difference between these video fragments and experienced action. In this variant of visual realism the equivalent of a refiguring pictorial perspectivism was created by foregrounding selected body parts and actions, and backgrounding others. The narration of authoritative witnesses established the formal point-of-view of the spectator.

These fabrications provided the prosecution, the defense and the jury with an extraordinary prosthetic penetration to same extent that the subjective and sensorial side of violence undergone by King was eviscerated. The agency of the participants in the trial (King never testified in court) was based on sensory privileges that were denied to King from beating to verdict. As the accused policemen accounted for their actions that night, they re-viewed and re-cast their violence through the pseudo-exactitude of the technologized eye, thereby flattening the chasm between enactment and testimony (as re-enactment). The reediting of the video juxtaposed temporally and spatially distanced acts creating a perceptual apparatus of holistic space-time compression that extended to, and empowered, the courtroom vision and discourse of the defendants. By such means the defense was able to convert the video into a time-motion study in police efficiency.[17] Here is Sergeant Duke using the camera's eye to rationalize police violence and enhancing their visual capacities in the midst of collectively delivering over a hundred blows to King. He simply invents a semiotics of King's imminent aggression.

> The suspect has the hand flat on the ground. The arm appears to be cocked. His left leg appears to be bent, coming up in a kneeling position; it appears to be in a rocking position with the other arm flat on the ground in a pushing position. (Court Room Television Network 1992)

King is indicted through the mindless autonomy of his detached limbs.

When asked by the prosecution if he considered King to be an animal, Officer Powell replied that King "was acting like one . . . because of his uncontrollable behavior" (Court Room Television Network 1992). In other words, King was bestial to the extent that he could not feel and therefore could resist the baton blows. Animalistic anaesthesia to pain provided a negative aura that retroactively established the sensitized and almost humanistic application of "reasonable violence" by the police. The police and King were distributed along a graded sensory scale. It is the visual acuity of the police in assessing the impact of their own violence that separates them, in a Cartesian fashion, from their own bodies and actions, and which becomes a contributing factor in the jury's verdict. While King could not be reasonable or lawful because he was submerged in a resistant body, without senses and without corresponding judgment. Confronting this resistance the police endowed King with affectivity by exploring the levels of pain that could finally register the will of the state on his body.

Narcosis was the final ingredient in the racial stew used to make King's anaesthesia. The defendants testified to their certainty that King was under the influence of "PCP" at the time of his arrest. Yet no physical collaboration was ever provided for this assertion despite King's medical examination. The powerful combination of racial innuendo and cine-matic dismemberment forged the complicity of the jury in the subtrac-tion of King's senses. As one jury member declaimed after the trial:

> "I am thoroughly convinced as the others I believe, that Mr. King was in full control of the whole situation at all times. *He was not writhing in pain* [emphasis added]. He was moving to get away from the officers and he gave every indication that he was under PCP. "(Riley 1992b: 116)

King was drugged yet in control, he felt no pain because he was drugged, but was trying to escape through the massive cordon of police that sur-rounded him with baton blows that he could not feel. The reciprocal can-cellation of these assertions could only be evaded through the alliance of sub-textual racist stereotypes and an equally fictitious, and decontextual-izing, micrological optic. Such statements attest to the juridical probity that informed the verdict. Another jury member was able to deliver an auteur theory of the Rodney King movie ". . . King was directing all the action . . . [he] was choosing the moment when he wanted to be hand-cuffed" (Riley 1992b: 116). King drugged and knocked prostrate to the ground from which he tries to crawl upward, presides over the violence to such an extent that it becomes self-inflicted and self-authored.

The defendant's testimony (with the exception of Brisenio) smuggled the authorial site of violence from the police and planted it on the victim. This was *embodiment by directed mimesis,* and a classic Lacanian "mirror relation" in which an imagined and specular Other is endowed with ideological attributes by the originating and dissimulating subject who provides the raw material of the refraction thereby covertly restaging it-self in that Other (Lacan 1977). Through racist transcription, the aggres-sion originating in the model (the police), became the qualifying somatic attribute of the copy (King). In transferring the origins of their violence to King, the police inhabit and possess his body in an imaginary relation where the black body becomes protective camouflage for state aggres-sion. Police violence was a *reenactment* of the violence "known" to be there in King's body. By this mimetic logic King was the magnetized pole attracting, soliciting and therefore animating the bodies of the police.

The conversion of King from the terminus to the source of aggression was enabled by a series of iconic displacements that embodied him in tandem with the disembodiment of police violence. Blackness, bestiality, narcosis and anaesthesia created the specularization of King's body. King, once invested with these mythemes functioned like a neo-colonial mirror that radiated an autonomous racial miasma that pre-justified state violence. Stretched out on the rack of distorted cinematic time and space, King's body could be described by Sergeant Duke as "a *spectrum* [emphasis added] of aggressive movements" (Court Room Television Network: 1992). In the logic of the colonial mirror (Taussig: 1987), the body to be colonized is defaced by myth and violence in order to turn it into an empty vessel that can serve as repository for the cultural armature and demonology of the colonizer (Feldman 1991c). By fashioning the murky density of the Other, the colonial regime succeeds in dematerializing and purifying its own violence in a crucial hegemonic displacement. The colonized mirror creature, through specular, becomes 'real' and laden with a negative material gravity in an exchange where the violence of the colonizer becomes spiritualized, i.e., made rational and lawful. The dematerialization of state violence by perceptual technologies contributed to the legitimacy of Operation Desert Storm and was also an important dynamic in the Simi Valley court room as indicated by one juror "They [the jury] didn't think much damage had been done to King as they looked at the photos [that displayed his bruises]." (Riley 1992b: 5)

*   *   *

> Three little girls were playing tag in the living room, a small white dog was barking happily and Sgt. Stacy Koon was rolling around on the rug, demonstrating the actions of the man who was beaten, Rodney G. King . . . The large screen television set dominates his living room, and Sergeant Koon cannot seem to stay away from it . . . "There's 82 seconds of use-of-force on this tape, and there's 30 frames per second," he said. "There's like 2,500 frames on this tape and I've looked at every single one of them not once but a buzillion times and the more I look at the tape the more I see in it . . . When I started playing this tape and I started blowing it up to 10 inches like I'd blow it up on this wall . . . fill up the whole wall . . . and all of a sudden, this thing came to life! . . . You blow it up to full size for people, or even half size, if you make Rodney King four feet tall in that picture as opposed to three inches, boy you see a whole bunch of stuff . . . He's like a bobo doll . . . Ever hit one? Comes back and forth, back and forth . . ." (Mydans, 1993: A14)

In this startling interview with Koon, he appears to be taken over by, and obsessed with the video. Through such reenactements as described above, he creates a physically mimetic bond with King's iconic body. Here, Koon uses his own body to reenact King's. It is my suggestion that this ex post facto simulation not only reflects and extends racial fictions and other constructions in Koon's courtroom testimony, but also derives from the actual police violence that, with each baton blow, inflicted a mythic black-bestial body on King's. When Sergeant Stacey Koon rolls around on his living room floor imitating, without sensory pain or shock, the man he has beaten, he merely plays the black body that was always his own. This play, so reminiscent of the child's improvizations before the

Lacanian mirror icon testifies to that inversion in the (neo-) colonial mirror relation when the possessor becomes the possessed (see Lacan 1977; Taussig 1987). Mimetic possession extends also to the somatic/technological interface. Sergeant Koon's quasi-visceral replay of that night is also a human mimicry of the video's capacity for flashback, fast forward and freeze frame. Sergeant Koon's body and memory have now become the screen upon which the video is played and replayed "back and forth" like a "bobo doll."

*   *   *

To critique cultural anaesthesia is not to assume that there can be a one to one correspondence of the senses to external things. Because that formula is infected with the rationality of objectivism and realism, which historically achieved such perceptual adequations through artifice and fictional supplements. Likewise, in the case of Rodney King, there could and should not be a return to the pristine originary event in-itself. That realism was argued for by the defense via the factotum of the partible video and by the prosecution who cited the video unpartitioned. Both parties argued for the video, in one form or another, as the true structure of the event and thereby banished with minor exceptions, the pre-event and post-event narrative framing of racist myth. Within the canon of realism, the video lens was truer than the human eye and absorbed the latter, because it could be sectioned and rationalized by time codes, slow motion, fast forward and freeze frame. The video's optic, as reworked by legal argument, epitomized realism's certitude of one to one relations between observer and observed precisely because its electronic prosthetics could be subjected to "realist" dissection and observation (see Crary 1991).

Though the defense had initially challenged the prosecution's video as exhaustive depiction, it then proceeded to insert another cinematic framing device, the authoritative voice-over narrative of police experts and the defendants. Endowed with a soundtrack the video was brought to cinematic completion and the jury was given the pleasure of narrative closure and a sense of an ending. As the video and its narrative grafts became the event, Rodney King was deleted from the courtroom and from the video as a legal personality. In their courtroom performance the once shadowy figures of the police stepped off the screen and appeared and spoke in the flesh, while the mute black figure remained incarcerated by the video and by violence. King only existed at the moment of violence, only in relation to material disorder, never in relation to language, memory, explanation, emotion and reason as did the policemen when they testified; these mediations distanced the police from King's pure physicality.

I began by reflecting on the hierarchy of those who entertain a social and perceptual distance from the body over those who are made to appear as captives of static materiality. This stratification organizes long-standing and seductive strategies for narrating the Other. Jural formalism, acceded to culturally mediated criteria of material evidence, and welcomed both unexamined racial and cinematic metaphors of embodied evil; it also gravitated to a technological formalism that enforced perceptual myths for the police and sensory muteness for their victim. Silent premises surrounded the trial which the court proved incapable of admitting: archaeologies of racial violence, cinematic rhetoric, the cultural bias of public memory and perception.

Salvaging sensory alterity in this context would not be a turn to a new realism that could compete with cinematic and legal realism, rather, as *re-perception*, it would recover relativizing materialities, stratigraphies of pain, and the historical limits, manipulative omissions and sanitizing censors of racial, media and juridical realism. Sensory deviation can and must leak through cultural censors as did the ambient distress of the Croatian folklorist in that conference hall. Bearers of sensory alterity have no option but to recover truth in a history of sensory fracture and dispersal which can be re-perceived as the dialogical ground for emergent cultural identities (see Seremetakis 1991a: 1–5). Here truth as fragment and as situated by a world of material discontinuity is the only counterpoint to the conflation of truth with the simulation of totality which elevates the societal capacity to mass produce facts to the ownership of history itself.

When normative institutional procedures, practices and depictions achieve literality and truth through the denial of their own material consequences and other people's sensory inscription, hegemony is created and forms of political consent are elicited which bar the Other from being present at the tribunal of historical actuality. Under these circumstances, violence, rather than being withdrawn by state monopoly, invisibly merges with vernacular experience. Sensory colonization brought about by the articulation of state culture, the media and the perceptual mythologies (racial, ethnic and gendered) of modernity, interdicts the structure of the everyday as a semi-autonomous zone of historical possibility and life chances. State, legal and media rationality, separately or combined, can erect a *cordon sanitaire* around disseminating public violence to the same extent that they successfully infiltrate social perception to neuter collective trauma, to subtract victims and to install public zones of perceptual amnesia which privatize and thus incarcerate historical memory. In this atomized context *"the memory of the senses"* (Seremetakis 1991b) becomes a vital repository of historical consciousness, and once shared and exchanged, the basis for illicit cultural identities.

Contrapuntal sensory histories can be located in the scattered wreck-
age of the inadmissible: lost biographies, memories, words, pains and
faces which cohere into *a vast secret museum of historical and sensory absence.* Rodney King was the absent, the invisible man at the trial that exposed his body to the exhaustive optics of advanced technology and racial conclusion. This established his sensory kinship with the Iraqis
whose deaths were electronically deleted from the American conscience.
King not only disappeared, but was provided with a surrogate, a stand-
in, through the mirror dynamics of projected racial aura and ideological
displacement. The defendants and their counsel transformed the Simi
Valley courtroom into a transvestite minstrel theater, where whites
armed with special effects and archetypal narratives, donned black face,
wore blacks masks, mimed a black body and staged a shadow play of
domination and law.[18]

Notes

1. As heard by the author on National Public Radio "All Things Considered"
on July 15, 1992.

2. The Croatian folklorist shall remain anonymous as she has the right to have
her research received independently of my perceptions of how and why she presented or performed her work as she did (See below). I confirmed many of my
interpretations of the talk and the audience's response in private conversation
with her. For similar reasons I will not impose on the hospitality of my Swedish
hosts by specifying the formal details of the conference. "Sweden" here functions
more as a metaphor of the European or Western metropole than as an actual place
as my argument will make clear.

3. See Feldman (1991a) for a discussion, in Northern Ireland, of the state's role
in integrating paramilitarism with popular Loyalist political culture, circa
1921–1972. Analogous state practices of democratizing violence by promoting
community-based confessional vigilante and/or paramilitary organizations
characterizes the escalatio of so-called resurgent ethnic violence in ex-Yugoslavia.
In both cases the state's complicity in the refashioning of ethnic identifications
through democratized violence, and the militarization of public culture, indicates
the expanding capacities of the state for the micro-management of everyday life
structures. These patterns call into question simplistic models of the "return of
the repressed" in relation to contemporary ethnic resurgence and aggression.

4. Though I later confirmed many of these perceptions and those that follow
with the Croatian folklorist, my responses at the time of her talk also reflected my
own unreconciled fieldwork experience in Belfast.

5. I am thinking here of the gendered inflections of ritual mourning in southern Europe (Seremetakis 1991a) as well as the work of Hélène Cixoux (1983).

6. In recent anthropological discourse the term "Other" has been assumed to
apply solely to a member of another discrete culture or subculture. But in Hegelian, existentialist, and Lacanian theory the term denotes relational social forms

within the same society without excluding its cross-cultural application. The use of the term in this paper is not meant to imply some essentialistic, fixed, homogenous, or ahistorical condition of an ethnic, religious or gendered group. The Other is a plural relation and not a monadic entity. This relation emerges from situated practices of domination and social violence. The term is not meant to imply a uniform category, insofar as uniformity itself is an element of the apparatus of domination, nor is the condition of Otherhood confined to complementary binary oppositions. It may be thought of as analogous to Robert Hertz's notion of the "left hand" or side: that which can never be definitively named. It is the heterogeneity and instability that mark the limits of monological power as much as it stands for the political aggression of certain acts of naming.

7. Though in instances pain itself can be objectified and become an object of cultural consumption in which its subjective or non-commodifiable dimensions would still be excluded.

8. See Williams (1991: 57–58) on the connection between race and sensory inadmissibility in contestation situations.

9. Fabian (1983), Stoller (1989), Tyler (1987) and Seremetakis (1991b) have presented significant discussions of the impact of sensory specialization and stratification on ethnographic perception. The relationship between state violence and sensory manipulation is analyzed in Feldman (1991a: 123–37).

10. The concept of historical perception used here is, of course, not limited to textual or even linguistic genres, forms and practices. It also implies that historical perception is always a re-perception.

11. Foucault's (1978) well known model of penological visual domination and training, inspired by Bentham's panopticon, frequently refers to the perceptual contributions of proscenium staging and back lighting to cellular surveillance.

12. Kojéve (1969) demarcates the Hegelian master from the slave or bondsman in terms of the former's exclusive engagement with consumption and the latter's immersion in labor. This implies normative sensualization of the master's body and punitive desensualization of the slave's body through alienated labor.

13. *From the Rodney King Case: What the Jury Saw in California versus Powell.* (Courtroom Television Network, 1992)

14. Much of this unfinished history tends to find expression in violent reenactments of the initiation, ritualized entry or processing of racial Others by the dominant institutions of white society.

15. Harvey (1989) refers to the reciprocal defining powers of marking certain urban zones as defiling and transgressive as does Williams (1991). This wilderness imagery, which obscures the particularities of community context from which racial others are subtracted, may well be a devolved variation of what Patterson (1982) identifies as "natal alienation." Natal alienation encompasses the renaming, branding and degradation practices in enslavement scenarios, and may still be a symbolic moment in the "Americanization" of racial others including African-Americans.

16. See Feldman (1991a: 81–84) on the political relation between animal imagery and violence.

17. There is a strong analogy between this re-editing of the video and Lukács' (1971) description of the bifurcation of the body of the assembly-line worker into

productive, commodifiable parts and actions and unproductive, economically devalued and "irrational" gestures. From this vantage point the link between the defense's version of the video and the freeze-frame time-motion photography of Fordist theoreticians is clear. The defenses discourse on reasonable police violence is the indirect heir of labor-efficiency performance analysis (see Rabinbach 1990).

18. In *Black Skin, White Masks* (1986), Frantz Fanon identified transvestitism as an essential element of the consciousness of the colonized. I am suggesting that it is crucial to the political prosthetics of the colonizer once the ideological and hegemonic power of the colonial mirror relation is considered.

References

Adorno, Theodor. 1973. *Negative Dialectics.* Translated by E.B. Ashton. New York: Continuum.

Bloch, Ernst. 1990. *Heritage of Our Times.* Cambridge Mass: MIT Press.

Cixous Hélène. 1983. "The Laugh of Medusa," In *The Signs Reader: Women, Gender and Scholarship.* Elizabeth Abel and Emil Abel, eds. Chicago: The University of Chicago Press.

Corbin, Alain. 1986. *The Foul and the Fragrant: Odor and the French Social Imagination.* Translated by M. Kochan, R. Porter and C. Pendergast. Cambridge, Mass: Harvard University Press.

Court Room Television Network. 1992. "The Rodney King Case: What the Jury Saw in California versus Powell." New York: Court Room Television Network.

Crary, Jonathan. 1991. *Techniques of the Observer: On Vision and Modernity in the Nineteenth Century.* Cambridge, Mass: MIT Press.

Elias, Norbert. 1982. *State Formation and Civilization.* Translated by Edmund Jephcott. Oxford: Basil Blackwell.

Fabian, Johannes. 1983. *Time and the Other: How Anthropology Makes Its Object.* New York: Columbia University Press.

Fanon, Frantz. 1986. *Black Skin, White Masks.* Translated by Charles Lam Markman. London: Pluto Press.

Feldman, Allen. 1991a. *Formations of Violence: The Narrative of the Body and Political Terror in Northern Ireland.* Chicago: The University of Chicago Press.

———. 1991b. "Collage and History: Max Ernst, Ernst Bloch, Walter Benjamin and the Ethnography of Everyday Life" (manuscript).

———. 1991c. "The Automaton, the Body and the Commodity Form: Sensory Hierarchies and Mimetic Others in Modernity." Paper presented at the Annual Meeting of the American Anthropological Association. Chicago, Illinois.

Foucault, Michel. 1978. *The Eye of Power.* Semiotext 3 (2):6–9.

Harvey, David. 1989. *The Condition of Postmodernity: An Enquiry into the Origins of Cultural Change.* Oxford: Basil Blackwell.

Heller, Joseph. 1961. *Catch 22.* New York: Modern Library.

Jameson, Federic. 1981. *The Political Unconscious: Narrative as a Socially Symbolic Act.* Ithaca: Cornell University Press.

Kojéve, Alexandre. 1969. *Introduction to the Reading of Hegel: Lectures in the Phenomenology of the Spirit.* Ithaca: Cornell University.

Lacan, Jacques. 1977. *Écrits: A Selection.* New York: W.W. Norton.

Lukács, Georg. 1971. *History and Class Consciousness: Studies in Marxist Dialectics.* Translated by Rodney Livingstone. Cambridge, Mass: MIT Press.

Mydans, Seth. 1993. "Their Lives Consumed, Officers Await 2d Trial." *New York Times,* February 2, 1993: p A14.

Patterson, Orlando. 1982. *Slavery and Social Death: A Comparative Study.* Cambridge, Mass: Harvard University Press.

Rabinbach, Anson. 1990. *The Human Motor: Energy, Fatigue and the Origins of Modernity.* New York: Basic Books.

Riley, John. 1992a. "The King Trial: What the Judge and the Jury Saw and Heard that the Public Didn't." *New York Newsday,* May 13, 1992: 17 and 30.

―――. 1992b. "The King Trial: The Judge and the Jury." *New York Newsday,* May 14, 1992: 5 and 116.

Scott, Paul. 1978. *The Day of the Scorpion.* New York: Avon Books.

Seremetakis, C. Nadia. 1991a. *The Last Word: Women, Death and Divination in Inner Mani.* Chicago. The University of Chicago Press.

―――. 1991b. "The Memory of the Senses: Historical Perception, Commensal Exchange and Modernity." Paper presented at the panel "The Anthropology of the Senses and European Modernity," in the American Anthropological Meetings, Chicago, 1991. Published in *Visual Anthropology Review,* vol.9, no.2, 1993, and in *Visualizing Theory,* edited by Lucien Taylor. New York: Routledge, 1994.

Stam, Robert. 1991. "Mobilizing Fictions: the Gulf War, the Media and the Recruitment of the Spectator." *Public Culture,* Vol. 4, No. 2, Spring 1991.

Stoller, Paul. 1989. *The Taste of Ethnographic Things: the Senses in Anthropology.* Philadelphia: University of Pennsylvania Press.

Taussig, Michael. 1987. *Shamanism, Colonialism and the Wild Man: A Study in Terror and Healing.* Chicago: The University of Chicago Press.

Tyler, Stephen. 1987. *The Unspeakable: Discourse, Dialogue and Rhetoric in the Postmodern World.* Madison: University of Wisconsin Press.

Williams, Patricia J. 1991. *The Alchemy of Race and Rights.* Cambridge, Mass: Harvard University Press.

7

"Conscious" Ain't Consciousness: Entering the "Museum of Sensory Absence"

Paul Stoller

"The Important thing is making generations. They can burn papers but they can't burn conscious, Ursa. And that's what makes evidence. And that's what makes the verdict."
—Gayl Jones's character
Great Gram in Corregidora

Gayl Jones's novel *Corregidora* is a haunting tale about cultural memory, about the "counter-memories" of four generations of African-American women. Throughout the novel the protagonist's great grandmother talks repeatedly about "conscious," and how the memories of "conscious" are deeper than the "official" historical texts and records. In this tale "conscious," which Great Gram considers "evidence," is sedimented in the bodies of four generations of black women, all of whom are haunted by the hulking presence of a Portuguese sailor who settled in Louisiana. Corregidora fed his lust by buying and possessing beautiful black women, including the women of Ursa's family. According to documents, Corregidora had legitimately employed these women. The documents make no mention of his whoring, pimping and incestuous rages. But Great Gram's story tells a different tale: one of sexual slavery, one of the persistent memories of incest and emotional abuse. Even Ursa and her mother, neither of whom had ever known Corregidora, were haunted by his presence. His hulking image torments their collective cultural memory, itself constituted by the invisible history of male sexual abuse. The following passage dramatically exemplifies cultural memory as a fundamentally embodied phenomenon:

... The two women in that house. The three of them at first then when I was older, just the two of them, one sitting in a rocker, the other in a straight-backed chair, telling me things. I'd always listen. I never saw my mama with a man, never ever saw her with a man. But she wasn't a virgin because of me. And still she was heavy with virginity. Her swollen belly with no child inside. And still she never had a man. Or never let me see her with one. No, I think she never had one ... When I was real little, Great Gram rocking me and talking. And still it was as if my mother's whole body shook with that first birth and memories and she wouldn't make others and she wouldn't give those to me, though she passed the other ones down, the monstrous ones, but she wouldn't give her own terrible ones. Loneliness, I could feel it, like she was breathing it, like it was all in the air. Desire, too, I couldn't recognize it then. But now when I look back, that's all I see. Desire and loneliness. A man that left her. Still she carried their evidence, screaming fury in her eyes ... (Jones 1986: 101–02)

But the memories of abuse and abandonment extend well beyond those of Ursa's mother and her pre-ordained fate with men. The fury and sadness also infused Ursa's voice, especially when she sang the blues at Happy's Club.

... Sometimes I wonder about their desire, Grandma's and Great Gram's. Corregidora was theirs more than hers. Mama could only know, but they could feel. They were with him. What did they feel? You know how they talk about hate and desire. Two humps on the same camel? Yes, hate and desire both riding them, that's what I was going to say. "You carry more than his name, Ursa," Mama would tell me. And I knew she had more than memories. Something behind the eyes. A knowing, a feeling of her own. But she'd speak only their life. What was their life, then? Only a life spoken to the sounds of the Victrola ... Still there was what they never spoke ... what they would even tell me. How all but one of them had the same lover? Did they begrudge her that? Was that their resentment? There was something ... They squeezed Corregidora into me, and I sung back in return (Jones 1986: 103).

Between the lines of her eloquent prose, Gayl Jones suggests that the power of collective memory does not merely devolve from textual inscriptions—a modernist conceit. It stems from stories (the oral tradition); it emerges from somewhere behind the eyes; it is squeezed from the sound-pain of the blues. For Gayl Jones, collective memories are evoked through the senses, from sentiments so elemental that they are beyond words, beyond the constraints of the text. When Ursa sings the blues, cultural memory possesses her. Her singing is therefore body-felt.

What can Ursa teach us about the essays in *The Senses Still*? What can Ursa's singing the blues teach us about the anthropology of perception and material experience in European modernity? The Ursas of the world remind us, first and foremost, that perception devolves not only from the visual surfaces of textual bodies, but from the depths of sentient sounds and the contours of repulsion/desire evoked by tastes and smells. The Ursas of the world, long consigned to the margins of social and intellectual life—to the domain of counter-memory—set a standard against which we can attempt to judge the faithfulness, if not the relevance, of our often errant wanderings in the vacuum between the intelligible and the sensible.

The Eyes of the World Are upon Us

Film theorists have long discussed the revolutionary potential of the cinema. In the early Soviet Union, as Susan Buck-Morss suggests in her essay, the cinema was seen as the most important political-ideological tool of Lenin's revolution. In France, surrealists, especially the early Artaud, also saw the cinema as revolutionary, but on a philosophical rather than a political plain. Theorists have also debated how the cinema altered perception. Much has been written on how audiences jumped in reaction to the screen arrival of a train in the Lumière brothers's first film, *L'Arrive d'un train dans la gare de Ciotat* (1895). Eisenstein (1975) believed that the filmmaker framed the perception of the audience. Bazin and Mitry believed in a more phenomenologically interactive theory of cinematic perception. Still others have looked to the cinema to ponder the relationship between image and desire, feminism and semiotics (de Lauretis 1984), feminism and psychoanalysis (Penley 1989), Theory and fiction (de Lauretis 1987) film image and language (Metz 1971; Hodges 1991). One of the most philosophically rigorous studies of film is that of Gilles Deleuze. In his two-volume work, *Cinema*, he discusses, among other matters, the perceptual intricacies of cinematic movement: framing, montage, action images, time images, thought and cinema.

Although Deleuze's cogitations on taxonomies of the cinematic image are intellectually breathtaking, they describe abstractly the unique sensuousness of the cinema. Left out of this analysis is the tactility that Walter Benjamin brought to the analysis of visual perception (see Taussig 1993; Buck-Morss 1989). It is in the space of visual sensuousness that Susan Buck-Morss delves philosophically and sensually into the cinema screen as a prosthesis of perception, an analysis which cuts beneath the surface of business-as-usual textual analysis to explore the somatic impact of cinematic images.

Buck-Morss begins, oddly enough, with Husserl's phenomenological reduction, his *epochē*. Husserl's preoccupation, she writes, is ". . . with the philosophical eye, his strenuous attempt to 'inspect' mental acts until their essences can be purely, intuitively 'seen' as absolute and non-contingent . . ." She briefly describes the philosophical rigor associated with

Husserl's "apodetic" and "eidetic" reductions, perceptual moves that enable observers to "see" universal essences that constitute a given object. Husserl is often criticized for his putative mysticism:

> And yet it is not medieval mysticism that provides the most accessible route to Husserl's project. If we wish to have a vision of the pure object, this "self-given" "absolute datum," which is neither physical thing nor psychological fact but (—wondrous phrase!—) an "intentionally inexistent entity", we would do best to put down the text, leave the lecture, and go to the movies.

Indeed, at the movies one sees the apodetically reduced object of cognition. "It is 'absolute data grasped in purely immanent seeing' in which we 'directly inspect the unity of cognition and object.' It is cognition that 'sees itself.'"

At first audiences were incapable of making the phenomenological reductions necessary to apprehend the cinematic image. For them, the cinema screen did not exist; they jumped at the sight of an oncoming train; they panicked at the sight of smiling severed head. Buck-Morss argues that "it took a certain transformation of the senses" for people to apprehend the cinema screen. Indeed, Buck-Morss suggests that the "surface of the cinema screen functions as an artificial organ of cognition. The prosthetic organ of the cinema screen does not merely duplicate human cognitive perception, but changes its nature." In other words,the cinema is able to project universal images that are synesthetic shocks to the senses. It is through the cinema that audiences become sensually aware of large collectivities: traffic in cities, street demonstrations, or, as in Eisenstein's films, the "masses" as the prime agents of change in significant historical events. Clearly, the apprehension of war and the mass appeal of violence devolve from the prosthetic intracacies of the cinema screen (Virilio 1989).

It is by way of the cinema screen, Buck-Morss tells us, that we can recognize what Ursas of the world know all too well: that cognition is physical. The Surrealists recognized the sensual power of the cinema screen. Artaud and Desnos, among others, realized that human beings are lulled into accepting the reality of the images in films and dreams, that human beings "misrecognize," following the terminology of Lacan and Williams, the illusion of the image (Williams 1981; Stoller 1992b). As a result, the scenarios of Artaud and Desnos attempt to construct films that would deconstruct our fundamental relationship to the cinematic image. These experiments failed for the most part; their power paled in comparison to sensual power of the cinematic image. Indeed, the cinematic image, manipulated through framing, close-ups, and montage, not only transforms our senses, but heightens them. "They expose the nerve endings to extreme stimulation of the most shocking physical sensations: violence and torture, the terrifying and catastrophic, the tantalizing and erotic," as Buck-Morss states.

Buck-Morss's analysis begs the question of how filmmakers, especially ethnographic filmmakers, should compensate for the sensual terror that the cinematic image can present. Many of the films of Jean Rouch display a healthy respect for the sensual power of cinematic image. Like his Surrealist mentors, Rouch uses film to provoke his audience. By the same token he is fully aware of the power of the mass appeal of cinematic images. He therefore makes films in collaboration with those whom he films. In the case of his classic, *Les Maitres Fous* (1956), one of the most provocative ethnographic films ever made, Rouch prudently limited distribution for fear of racist interpretation. And no wonder. The film includes scenes of spirit-possessed black Africans handling fire, frothing at the mouth, drinking blood gushing from a freshly slaughtered dog, chomping on dog meat, and all the while imitating Europeans. These images overwhelmed the subtle philosophical themes embedded within and between the frames of the film (Stoller 1992a). Are other ethnographic filmmakers equally sensitive to the sensual power of the cinematic image? The message that Buck-Morss is sending to anthropological image makers is that they must not forget their ethical and political responsibilities in a world in which the intelligible power of the text has been eclipsed by the sensible power of the image. Image makers have the power to sensually excite the audience; they also have the capacity to condition audiences into chewing endlessly on the pablum of what Renato Rosalado calls "imperialist nostalgia." The widespread proliferation of the *Millennium* series on North American television and in video stores underscores the wisdom of Buck-Morss's message.

Swedish Bodies

The contribution of Jonas Frykman on the social construction of the Swedish body in the 1930's underscores Buck-Morss's point about the universal appeal of mass images. It is a potent demonstration of the curiously modernistic link of hypersensitivity and anaesthesia. Frykman argues that the sensory revolution that reconfigured the Swedish body also reconfigured the Swedish body politic—into the much admired modern welfare state. Indeed, admiring commentators have long suggested the relationship between healthy bodies and healthy body politics.

Frykman analyzes links among local practices, cultural identity and national politics in Sweden. Following Foucault, he argues that power comes from below. The transformation of Sweden from a relatively backward agrarian nation into the model of the modern welfare state, he writes, stems from local social movements that embodied the themes of modernism. The political transformation, which dates to the 1930s, devolved, in part, from the Swedish penchant for exercise—gymnastics. "Gymnastics must be understood in the light of the inter-war delight for *doing*, in *showing*, and *talking about* what had previously been inconceivable or secret." The enthusiasm for the new—the credo of modernism— was expressed not only through gymnastics, but through vegetarianism, nudism, and athleticism. The new sensuality in Sweden corresponded to a new sexual openness, which was articulated "on the pages of contemporary books, on the silver screen, on the bandstands and the couches." This articulation expressed the mass appeal of personal conquest. If one could conquer her or his body, one could meet the future and master it.

Frykman situates the transformation of the Swedish body in Swedish space. Swedes had to conquer their bodies outdoors, breathing in fresh air as they toned their muscles. The air of the city, of course, was not up to the standards set for bodily conquest; one had to repair to the countryside, to pristine lakes and unspoiled mountains. From one's experience in the country, one could learn about living, about perfecting individual practices. Life in the countryside was simple, uncluttered, clear, natural, rational. Indeed, the transformation of Swedish bodies was soon linked to the promotion of a worthy and reasonable life, which had its Swedish roots in Lutheran piety.

Frykman goes on to describe how the Social Democrats tapped this local ferment for fitness to engineer the welfare state. "The citizens of the Swedish welfare state—'the home for the people'—were subjected to well-meaning attempts at colonization by people who knew how they should organize their day-to-day life and look after their bodies." This experiment exacted a price, according to Frykman: Ordinary citizens deferred to the wisdom of those who knew best. Although Frykman only hints at how the state constructed its imagery, there is little doubt that it exercised an incredibly powerful influence over individual will, an "aristocracy of intelligence," to use Frykman's language, to ". . . replace all previous nobility—the nobility that relied on violence, birth, or wealth."

Viewed from Buck-Morss's vantage, the transformation of the Swedish body and body politic seems like a very successful case of national anaesthetization. This change, as Frykman demonstrates, came from below—at first. But the movement for change was soon co-opted by reform minded middle class intellectuals, who, in effect, colonized the already transformed Swedish body. Reading Frykman one gets the impression of a nation of contented citizens who follow those who know best; one gets the impression that Swedes had left behind the zesty subjectivities of Great Gram's "conscious" in favor of the bland objectivities of consciousness. Difference is obliterated as Swedish subjects are incorporated into the objectivized body politic. The celebrated success of the Swedish social experiment is today a cautionary example; it forces us to recognize the power of state image-making, the power of the state to objectify difference, to excise the discordant, to shape its dominance.

Electronic Anaesthesia

In her contribution to *The Senses Still*, Susan Buck-Morss suggests that when confronted by the cinema, the nervous system is modified in a seemingly paradoxical way: "On the one hand there is an extreme heightening of the senses, a hypersensitivity of nervous stimulation. On the other, there is a dulling of sensation, a numbing of the nervous system that is tantamount to corporeal anaesthetization." Frykman's article gives us an example of how the reorganization of the senses in Sweden resulted in the objectification of individual corporeality and the anaesthetization of the body politic by those "who knew best." Enter Alan Feldman who, in his contribution to this volume, describes how the state is able to manipulate visual images to erase that which might stimulate us to resist, how the state dulls us into blithely accepting the unacceptable.

Feldman defines cultural anaesthesia as "the banishment of disconcerting, discordant and anarchic sensory presences and agents that undermine normalizing and often silent premises of everyday life." This take on cultural anaesthesia devolves from Adorno who suggested that in late modernity the "quantitative and qualitative increase of objectification increases the social capacity to inflict pain on the Other—and I [Feldman] would add—to render the Other's pain inadmissible to public discourse and culture." Based upon Adorno's insight, Feldman calls for politically sensitive anthropology of the senses and suggests that sensory capacities are not evenly distributed in complex societies with crosscutting sectors of economic, racial, ethnic, gender and cultural domination. Since the time of Plato and Aristotle, the senses, which have long been specialized and stratified, have been used by the Republic to legitimate the authority of the few. But the exponential stratification and specialization of the senses in modernity becomes especially poignant when we consider the potency of cinematic and other visual images and the power of the media and the State to sanitize them.

Cultural anaesthesia is, in fact, a direct descendant of realism. In the nineteenth century, Feldman points out, realism presupposed an omniscient observer who visualized reality through his narrations. In such a space, time becomes linear, regular, homogenized, and the subject becomes just one more aspect of representation (Lowe 1982; Crary 1991). These cornerstones of scientific objectification become in the twentieth century part and parcel of burgeoning commodification, all of which transfers the discussion of the real from philosophical salons to the consumer airwaves—radio,the cinema, television, video. Such a transfer renders dear the power of the image, the symbol, the trademark (Coombe 1994). Through the sanitization of the consumer image, bodies are depersonalized; they are one among any number of realist objects, all of which are devoid of odors, distinction, and pain.

Feldman describes a stew of images that has no flavor, no odor, no texture—only a tasteless, depersonalized surface image. These images put us to sleep, make us listless, make us impervious to that which "doesn't fit" within the stylized scope of things. Such a stew of images, according to Feldman, disembodies the subject. Feldman powerfully demonstrates this process of symbolic evisceration through the descriptions of the air-brushed media coverage of Operation Desert Storm and the imageric disembodiment of Rodney King.

In Operation Desert Storm ". . . The eulogized smartbombs were prosthetic devices," writes Feldman, "that extended our participant observation in the video occlusion of absented Iraqi bodies . . . Their broadcast images functioned as electronic simulacra that were injected into the collective nervous system of the audience as antibodies that inured the viewer from realizing the human-material consequence of the war." Viewed from afar, the war became an entertaining light show that highlighted the technological wonders of military. "We" were cashing-in on the multi-billion dollar military investments of the Reagan years. Violence, death, and misery did not seep through the visual images. After all, as Ursa's Great Gram would say, those "negatives" had become part of the "conscious" rather than the consciousness of war.

Feldman's analysis of the Rodney King debacle demonstrates what happens when "conscious" slips into consciousness, violating the carefully constructed realism of commodified facticity. Initially, the images of Los Angeles police mercilessly beating a defenseless King shocked people in the United States. These were graphic images of state-sponsored violence or making pain, in Feldman's terms. No sanitized violence here. Initially, the image of King's brutal beating made him a subject-in-pain. But "conscious," as Ursa's Great Gram knew so well, is exceedingly dangerous, even seditious; it must be transformed into consciousness. And so the invisible image-makers set about to totally objectify the pain-suffering subject.

The first step in objectification was to bestialize Rodney King. As Feldman points out, King was referred to "bear-like," a being on his "haunches." Such objectification, to return to Adorno's point, augments the State's capacity to inflict pain. King is likened to an animal, symbolism that is consistent with longstanding racist imagery the history of which can be traced to Herotodus through Gobineau to the present (Miller 1985; Stoller 1992a). Incapable of language, the animal is silenced. Animals, moreover, do not feel pain. It is only "reasonable" for the policemen, who represent the State, to beat savage animals. To make matters worse, the police testified that King—or so they thought—was on PCP. And so the objectification of King—the sanitization of the violence brought upon his body—proceeds through the frames of blackness, bestiality, narcosis, and finally, anaesthesia.

"Conscious" in Feldman's language is "sensory alterity." He suggests that it is a high priority for social scientists to salvage "conscious" so as to compete with what he calls the realisms of the cinema and the law. Feldman's plea doesn't mean that anthropologists should naively "give voice" to the other. The role of the committed scholar, rather, is to locate "lost biographies, memories, words, pains and faces which cohere into a vast secret museum of historical absence." That is precisely the burden that Great Gram delivers to Ursa. When Great Gram says, that "they can burn papers but they can't burn conscious," she passes on to Ursa the burden of cultural memory. Ursa's burden is also that of contemporary anthropologists who must increasingly monitor the anaesthetizing ethers that the State continuously pulses into air.

Memories of the Senses

Feldman's analysis of cinematic and legal realism compels us to wonder where to find "conscious" amid the ever-more intricate netting of carefully constructed cultural camouflage. Feldman writes of lost biographies, words, gazes, and pains—an encyclopedia of "conscious." He also writes of a lecture given by an embattled Croatian anthropologist. Although this woman spoke of reflexive anthropology, there was something in her talk that seeped through the rarefied discourse of texts, heteroglossia, and ethnographic authority. Her presentation was "a palpable and gendered self-reflexivity that had been channeled by the sensory remembrance of scheduled terror." This anthropologist was unable to erase the grief from her voice, unable to untangle the knots of pain from her body. Unable to deal with pain and grief, the audience intellectualized the discussion. Confronted by the alien primitive, the audience in Sweden transformed the fragmented chaos of the sensible into the holistic order of the intelligible. In the Academy, after all, only a small number of savants want to deal with the sensible, with the "throwness" of the emotions.

The alienation of grief, pain, and other emotions has a long history dating—in print at least—to Plato's Republic. Plato, of course, recommended the banishment of poets and dramatists from his Republic.

Pandering to the heart's emotions, he reasoned, would upset the head's thoughts. And yet, poetry is the elemental language, the expression, par excellence, of the human imagination. It is a cache of sensory alterity, of "conscious." It is one door into what Feldman calls "the secret museum of historical absence."

In the papers by Buck-Morss, Frykman, and Feldman the authors use the language of the academy to rethink the configuration of the senses in modernity. They present arguments that use the logic of the Academy to subvert categories and assumptions. In her contribution C. Nadia Seremetakis employs the poetics of textual montage to fuse ethnographic description, cultural memory and the conceptual problematics of modernity. "The Memory of the Senses" is an artful essay that powerfully articulates the disciplinary benefits of adopting a more poetically sensual approach to ethnography.

Seremetakis structures chapter 3 as a play in six acts: Prelude, saliva, the journey, traffic, dust, and reflexive commensality. Like a good play, each act is but a fragment of a whole—ethnography—that is itself riven with faults and fissures. She writes that . . . "the use of montage here is not simply an aesthetic or arbitrary choice. Sensory and experiential fragmentation is the form in which this sensory history has been stored and this dictates the form of its reconstruction."

Seremetakis tells the story of the Greek grandma who feeds the Greek baby by chewing bread until it becomes a paste. Grandma then takes the bread from her mouth and puts it into the baby's mouth. In this way bread and saliva bind grandma and baby. In fact, metaphors of baking pervade Greek notions of socialization. "A woman raises a child as she raises dough into bread. Working the bread with the tongue and saliva, the grandma changes it to dough which is then used to raise the child." In other words, to bake is to be enculturated. By the same token social memory in Greece is baked/sung/smelt. Here Seremetakis underscores a fundamental flaw in much of the scholarly writing on the body. In most scholarly treatises, the body is considered a text that is "read" and "written." In Seremetakis's essay the body is neither exclusively "read" nor "written": it is also felt.

The memory of the senses, however, is never static. When one takes a trip in rural Greece, as described by Seremetakis, one's body is consumed by the world, by smells, by cultural memory:

> . . . Each smell generates its own textures and surfaces. No smell is encountered alone. There are combinations of smells that make up a unified presence, the gramdma's house: the garden aroma combined with the animal dung; the oregano bunch hanging over the sheep skin containing the year's cheese; the blankets stored in the cabinet which combine rough

wool with the humidity of the ocean; the oven exuding the smell of baking bread and the residue of ashes; the fresh bread in the open covered with white cotton towels.

Such a range of smells cannot be silenced. One can taste the various points on the journey from city to country. One can taste the seasons. Such descriptions cut to the heart of embodiment, a concept that many scholars understand only partially. Seremetakis's essay teaches us that embodiment is not textual. The human body is not principally a text; rather, it is consumed by a world filled with smells, textures, sights, sounds and tastes, all of which trigger cultural memories.

The sights, sounds, smells and tastes of Seremetakis's essay create a sensory context for her ruminations on "reflexive commensality." "Between grandmas and grandchild sensory acculturation and the materialization of historical consciousness occurred through the sharing of food, saliva, and body parts." For Seremetakis, this sharing produces a setting of commensality which she defines as ". . . the exchange of sensory memories and emotions, and of substances and objects incarnating remembrance and feeling." This path is one that leads us to the secret museum that Feldman evokes: the museum of sensory absence.

Of Dust and Anthropology

For much of its history anthropology has been a dusty discipline. History, of course, is renowned as *the* dusty discipline—all those years that historians spend amid the archival dust. Although increasing numbers of historically-minded anthropologists have experienced archival dust, the dustiness of anthropology is qualitatively different. In anthropology, dust reflects age, a condition which, in turn, valorizes *authenticity*. There is also in anthropology the ultimately unattainable quest for the culturally pristine—so artfully and painfully described in Levi-Strauss's *Tristes Tropiques*. Unable to obtain the unobtainable, anthropologists perfected the practice of "dusting off." Archaeologists have "dusted off" bones and pots to "expose" a "culture" complex. Based on "data" collected during fieldwork, cultural anthropologists have "dusted off" social structures, kinship systems, exchange systems, cognitive maps, symbolic inversions, domestic modes of production, transnational networks, and even postcolonial ethnoscapes:

When the anthropologist first enters the field site the sensory organization of modernity, the perceptual history and commensal structure of the discipline direct her/him to first see dust. Without long-term fieldwork and sensory archaeology the anthropologist may never come to know that this

dust is a surface residue of the researcher's own acculturation that obscures depth: other sensory surfaces that embody alternative materialities,
commensalities and histories. Without a reflexive anthropology of the
sense, fieldwork, short or long, remains trapped in the literal, captive of
realist conventions that are themselves unacknowledged historically determined perceptual and commensual patterns. This is well understood by
those who inhabit the memory of other sensory and material reciprocities.
How can they take anthropologists seriously if the latter go with the
dust?

As Seremetakis argues above, unreflexive dusting off not only cleans
an object of so much sedimentation, but also kicks up clouds that obscure
one's vision. Dusting off is part and parcel of a methodology that builds
what Seremetakis, Feldman, and Buck-Morss would call sensory anaesthesia. The images of cinema and the airwaves, as has been suggested in
this book, can create veritable dust storms that irritate our eyes, narrow
our nasal passages, clog our pores, swell our tongues and infect our ears.
These storms engulf us in clouds of dust that cut us off from sensory alterity, from embodied memories of pain, terror, love, loss, poetry, sensibility, grandmas and Great Grams, from memories of the secret history
hidden in the museum of sensory absence.

In the past anthropologists have, indeed, gone with the dust. In the
future perhaps we shall become "conscious" of a wind that blows in
more than one direction.

References

Buck-Morss, Susan. 1989. *The Dialectics of Seeing: Walter Benjamin and the Arcades
Project.* Cambridge, Mass.: MIT Press.

Coombe, Rosemary J. 1994. *Cultural Appropriations: Intellectual Property Laws,
Postmodern Culture and Late Modern Politics.* (Forthcoming from Routledge,
Chapman, and Hall.)

Crary, Jonathan. 1991. *Techniques of the Observer: On Vision and Modernity in the
Nineteenth Century.* Cambridge, Mass.: MIT Press.

Deleuze, Gilles. 1986. *Cinema 1: The Movement-Image.* Trans. Hugh Tomlinson and
Barbara Habberjam. Minneapolis: University of Minnesota Press.

————. 1989. *Cinema 2: The Time Image.* Trans. Hugh Tomlinson and Robert
Galeta. Minneapolis: University of Minnesota Press.

Eisenstein, Sergei. 1975. *The Film Sense.* Trans. Jay Leyda. New York: Harcourt,
Brace, Jovanovich.

Hedges, Inez. 1991. *Breaking the Frame: Film Language and the Experience of Limits.*
Bloomington, Indiana: Indiana University Press.

Jones, Gayl. 1986. *Corregidora.* New York: The Grove Press.

Lauretis, Teresa de. 1984. *Alice Doesn't: Feminism, Semiotic, Cinema.* Bloomington,
Indiana: Indiana University Press.

————. 1987. *Technologies of Gender: Essays on Theory, Film, and Fiction*. Bloomington, Indiana: Indiana University Press.

Levi-Strauss, Claude. 1956. *Tristes Tropiques*. Paris: Gallimard.

Lowe, Donald. 1982. *History of Bourgeois Perception*. Chicago: The University of
Chicago Press.

Metz, Christian. 1971. *Language et Cinema*. Paris: Larousse.

Miller, Christopher. 1985. *Blank Darkness: Africanist Discourse in French*. Chicago:
The University of Chicago Press.

Penley, Constance. 1989. *The Future of An Illusion: Film, Feminism, and Psychoanalysis*. Minneapolis: University of Minnesota Press.

Stoller, Paul. 1992a. *The Cinematic Griot: The Ethnography of Jean Rouch*. Chicago:
The University of Chicago Press.

————. 1992b. "Artaud, Rouch and the Cinema of Cruelty." *Visual Anthropology
Review* 8(2): 50–58.

Taussig, Michael. 1993. *Mimesis and Alterity: A Particular History of the Senses*.
New York: Routledge.

Virilio, Paul. 1989. *Cinema and War: The Logistics of Perception*. London: Verso.

Williams, Linda. 1981. *Forms of Desire*. Berkeley: University of California Press.

Films Cited

Lumiere, Louis. 1895. *L'Arrive d'un train a la gare de Ciotat*. Paris.

Rouch, Jean. 1956. *Les Maitres Fous*. Paris: Films de la Pleiade.

8

Implications

C. Nadia Seremetakis

Lost and Found

In the first decades of this century critical theorists such as Simmel, Benjamin, Bloch and the Surrealists, spoke of the senses in terms of the inundating experience of sensory flooding, shock and multiplicity. The loss of past sensory identities was frequently compared to the emergence of new modes of perception, new conditions of being an object and new identities of the perceiving subject. This theme was carried into the phenomenology of Merleau-Ponty who, at mid-century, saw sensorial exploration of the phenomenological life world of modernity as still crucial. Yet today the rare discussions of the senses focus directly or by allusion on the theme of loss, repression, exclusion, and alienation. In many ways these themes echo pseudo-Foucauldian perspectives that treat the body solely as a dematerialized textual object. What are the implications, but also the presuppositions of this exclusive focus? Have we lost the senses in modernity? Or to put it differently, has modernity lost the senses? And by extension, are we studying the Other to justify and/or to rectify our imputed loss?

To claim to have lost the senses, is to objectify them, to render them a discrete article that can be detached, then disposed of and eventually reappropriated. The directional and linear thrust of these characterizations tacitly emplot many inquiries into the senses. Yet this emplotment exudes an odor of the very same cultural postures and presuppositions that are blamed for effacing the senses in the first place; i.e., instrumental rationality, objectification, linearity, mind/body dualisms (the senses are alienable but still can be thought) and consumer-commodity culture. Thus the thematic of sensory loss can operate as an ahistorical and symptomatic plaint of the very cultural structures that are presented as desensitizing.

Sensory loss has been one concern of this volume as well. Yet, as I discuss later, the theme of loss does not have to imply directional and teleological closure, and such closures can serve to obscure the very sensory depth that is meant to be recovered. There is no one universal and culturally neutral way to deal with loss as the etymologies of the Greek word *nostaghía* showed. The semantic circuit of that word emphasizes the sensory dimensions of the experience of loss and the maturation process that occurs with an immersion into the material experience of estrangement. The term also implies that loss, estrangement, exile, temporal and spatial separation, are ongoing intrinsic and existential sensory-historical experiences, crucial to the cultural construction of memory. This is in contrast to the instrumental and linear premise of "that which is lost must be found" that underlies most theoretical investigations of the senses, and the body and materiality in general, and which implies that an anti-historical reunification must take place which reverses time. In contrast, the Greek etymology of sensory dislocation, memory and emotional re-immersion (as discussed in the first chapters) is unthinkable without the ontological connection of the sensory and the temporal. The sensory is always engaged with experiential deferment, thus it rarely evokes the notion of an anchoring originary and identity-conferring experience. Sensory identity in Greece is constructed in the midst of absence.

The cultural complicity of the thematic of loss and utopian recuperation within the experience of modernity, is rarely examined in the narratives that advance the search for the senses in alterity. Alterity has been treated as something outside of and beyond modernity; its narrative function is to be another name for evoking modernity's separation from a primal and originary sensory experience which now can be relocated in and recovered from a cultural or historical Other. The question remains: to what extent is this imputed sensory dimension of the Other merely a suppressed, exiled part of the sensory structure of modernity that is now smuggled into the analysis of the material experience of diverse cultures and historical periods?

To ask such a question is *not* to presume an alternative capacity to extract an untouched and pristine cultural and/or historical sensory depth from the Other. For that is to reify the sensorial within the Other in the very process of subtracting it from modernity. This is simply another symptom of modernity when one considers that to allocate a generic sensory expertise to one culture at the expense of another is to replicate the division and specialization of the senses which is one of the central myths and political forces of the modern. Here sensory segmentation moves from the monadic (individualized) body to entire societies which are treated as singular entities-in-themselves that acquire mutually exclusive sensory realities. This move also bars the Other from modernity by foreclosing the question of other present and possible modernities that can be counterpoints to the hegemonic modernity associated with the Euro-American metropole. Rather, the reflexive interplay of multiple sensory realities and their uneven and non-identical historical transformations must be attended to; though not always from the perspective and priorities of a culture that treats other cultures and epochs as insurance policies of its own vanished experience.

My intention is not to deconstruct in order to debunk the theory of sensory loss for the sake of intellectual debating only. After all, I share with that perspective a respect for alternative sensory systems which can constitute provisional refuge areas in the prevailing sensory cacophony of modernity. Searching for the senses in otherness is not objectionable. In fact it is critical. The important issue, however, is not to lose sight of how this search is carried out and what exactly is being looked for. When anthropologists and other cultural critics claim that they are in search of the senses they should first cope with the question: if modern-western embodiment has been desensitized, in what form can perceiving subjects from that context perceive the senses of the cultural other? Will that particular act of perception merely replicate the very violence against the senses that the western commentator seeks to escape from, to rectify and to compensate? To what extent "realist" descriptions of other sensory cultures, outside or within our own society, reduce and distill these realities to the material certitude that is felt to be lacking among the multiplicity of modernity?

To what extent does the allegorical code of realism deface intrinsic metaphorical dimensions in other sensory dispositions? (See discussion of Schneider and Weiner's work, below.) Is even the culturally relative depiction of the other sensory predilections compelled to reduce the latter to literalities precisely because within modernity the notion of direct material experience has fallen into semantic crisis? Has modernity undergone a destabilization, which can only be corrected by the imputed perceptual stability and sensory anchorage of other cultures?

Thus any discussion of the senses cannot be partitioned from a consideration of modernity; the two subjects are interwoven. The presuppositions that enter into any inquiry on the sensorial are apriori claims about modernity; and to search for the senses in another culture or another historical epoch is always to write the critical history of "our" own contemporary material experience.

*   *   *

The narrative of sensory loss is a subtext that engages certain stereotypical motifs and premises of questionable value. The subject of loss always speaks to the enticing theme of a fall, a debasement, a movement of high to low which immediately organizes any history into a teleology. The thematic of "the fall" also has its origins in earlier cultural narratives of the senses in which the loss of meaning is portrayed as a fall into debasing sensory experience. Thus the search for lost senses merely inverts this motif; a strategy that reinforces its symptomatic and binary character.

The suggested compensation for this experience of sensory closure is "re-opening" via sensory otherness and through comparative, and culturally relative classifications. A vital analytic lens of the comparative approach is the notion of relative sensory ratios or balances (for example Howes 1981). Cultures and historical periods are explored for their different sensory arrangements from the vantage point of a base-line analytic context from which comparisons can be made. The notion of ratio presumes that there are five originary, discrete senses which have different relations of dominance and subordination to each other. It can also accommodate situations in which other senses may be tacked on or from which items may be deleted. But this numerical concept already assumes a specialization of the senses and a literality of sensory capacities through the notion of an apriori divisibility of material experience (as in Tyler 1987). Enumerated sensory capacities and the corresponding segmentation of material experience into specialized semantic domains may freeze the actual fluidity of sensory crossing and mutual metaphorization of one sense by another, that can be encountered in Greek culture among others. Enumeration thus imposes an objectifying grid that distorts or effaces the manner in which a culture senses the senses, the meta-sensory yet equally material techniques that replicate perceptual experience as cultural form in time and space. Enumeration and sensory ratio, as facilitators of comparativity, may be "our" meta-techniques for the distillation of sensory experience. However, they infer a "natural" pre-cultural existence of the senses which undergoes subsequent cultural mutation. It is obvious how this notion of enumerated senses informs a narrative of sensory loss. Enumeration speaks to the notion of sensory quantification or holism that fixes the senses in time and space. Thus enumeration guarantees the ends of the search for lost senses by pre-arranging the object of eventual recovery. The numbering of the senses further permits the binary code of balance/imbalance which is crucial to teleological historical accounts. Balance/imbalance is merely another way of saying lost/ found, West/Other and permits all sorts of comparison from the perspective of a lack which can be filled up with positivity from other cultures.

Such distinctions authorize a theoretical objectification of the senses by one cultural site while denying the existence of complex and reflexive epistemologies of the senses at other cultural sites. "They" become lived experience and "we" are reasserted as thought and writing. The sensory conditions within western modernity that permit such dualisms, the extent to which this binaryism itself may be directed at the repression of aspects of sensory experience in western modernity, are not considered. Such cognitive operations on the sensory experience of others are also sensory operations on ourselves that facilitate the reproduction of internal histories (however this is rarely spoken of). In this manner the search for the senses becomes instrumentalist and carries with it covert rationalities—ratios, balance, holism, enumeration, limited thematic variation, realism, reductive materialism, mentalist norms—that facilitate the reductive comparison of radically different, though historically interacting sensory alterities. These postures automatically generate predetermined narrative sequences and it must be asked, what is the fate of sensory experiences and practices that are not admissible to the notions of balance, ratio and enumeration? The latter terms trace the mirrored play of cross-cultural power relations that advance the appropriation of the senses by one cultural site, while enabling the evasion of the sensory implications of that textualization itself.

The Politics of the Senses

Buck-Morss's essay begins with Husserl who approaches perception as an intuitive mental act that can be inspected by thought. At issue here, and the stumbling block to any universal "perceptualism," such as the phenomenological reduction, is the apprehension of the object as "given." Throughout this volume the dynamics of historical and sensory sedimentation render giveness, the unambiguous insertion of object in an ideal perceptual present, an impossibility.

Buck-Morss links the presumption of perceiving the object as given to the privileged position of vision in western modernity. This intersects with my contention in chapter 1, that literality and the giveness of perceptual objects is a historical construct predicated on the segmentation and partitioning of the senses. Thus, in a historically contextualizing slide, Buck-Morss moves from Husserl's idealized seeing to one of its echoes in the material culture of Husserl's epoch. At the movies, the illusion of a giveness to things is technologically constructed, through "acts of pure seeing."

Buck-Morss reads the fabrication of the literal ironically . Literal or fetishized vision is powerful and efficacious to the very same extent that it is imaginary and manufactures non-existent but ideologically necessary objects and realities; a point also made by Feldman in reference to the visually dissected body of Rodney King.

Buck-Morss's analysis of created cinematic objects brings into mind Jameson's (1981) point that the modern division of sensory labor should not only be seen from the perspective of fragmentation, loss, alienation and a mythical de-naturing of the body; rather sensory specialization in modernity opens up new worlds of vision and sensation such as abstraction in the arts, the aesthetic rehabilitation of everyday objects, or the imaginary "realism" of the life-worlds displayed on cinema screens. Crary (1991) has pointed out that a crucial cultural agenda in the division of the senses was the desire for cognition to see itself. Realism is legitimized by the capacity to subject perception and the senses to an objectivizing dissection: the instrumental seeing of perception. This too is posited as a pure act of reductive vision that is perceptually far superior and more exacting than its object, vernacular perception. The scientific and economic partitioning of the senses became the symbolic system by which sensory reality, and hence, everyday life experience is to be apprehended and recorded. Feldman's discussion of the Rodney King trials shows how this 19th century scientific discourse has been transmuted, in the present, into the legal criteria of visual evidence.

Both writers propose that sensory transformation is tied to how a society is allowed to depict the senses. Sensory hierarchy is first worked out in the selecting and privileging of modes of representation that have the senses as their specialized object. New sensory hierarchies require subtending by new modes of representing which can displace prior depictive cultures. Here the notion of the memory of the senses, the import of its attrition or transformation, is crucial to explaining how sensory experience "magically" disappears from history (see Corbin 1986). Forms of sensory depiction and their cultural displacement has to be understood here in its widest sense, including the narratives and iconography located within the talking objects of a signifying material culture.

Commensal practices discussed in my essay in chapter 3, use the material world as a meta-narrative on sensory experience. Sensory memory is encapsulated, stored and recuperated in these artifacts, spaces and temporalities of consumption, sharing and exchange. Yet, Buck-Morss and Feldman speak of how, in exemplary zones of western modernity, sensory experience is stored in and exclusively narrated by scientific, legalistic, medicalized discourses: the apparatuses of realism. How different edifices permit us to speak about the senses, culminates in sensory abstention, the unsayable and the forgettable. This dynamic connects the cultural formation of inattention in modernity to the stylization of sensory evidence and discourse.

Buck-Morss traces current sensory transformations to the cinematic violation of late 19th century perceptual reality. Capturing this historical shift is crucial, for today cinematic objects and seeing ultimately mediate, if not construct, our perception of the real—a point poetically sharpened by Jean Luc Godard in his recent three-part film *Histoire(s) du Cinéma*

(1989). Godard remembers this century through a dense montage of lost cinematic glances that cohere into a visual vernacular of everyday cinematic experience. In *Histoire(s) du Cinéma* the history of the 20th century cannot be disentangled from the 20th century history of cinematic perception. The event of each cinema frame and the visual framing of each historical event have become almost indivisible. As Feldman points out, the perception of history is the history of perception.

Both Godard's and Buck-Morss's works support my view in chapter 1, that perceptual memory as a cultural form, is not to be found in the psychic apparatus of a monadic, pre-cultural and ahistorical seer, but is encased and embodied out there in a dispersed surround of created things, surfaces, depths and densities that give back refractions of our own sensory biographies. The cinematic screen, understood as a layered archeological site is one such repository of sensory history. Buck-Morss speaks of it as a prosthetic organ, as if it was a detached, separable and yet collectivized part of each individual body. Godard, in *Histoire(s) du Cinéma*, films himself standing by an archival shelf of books, but can only recall and visualize (which is the same thing) the 20th century through the material mediation of the cinema screen. For him, the cinema screen is not a flat text-like surface that can be opened and closed and put away; rather it is a volume into which his own auto- and political biography is sunk; it is his Aphrodite's peach, an organ of memory made palpable. Thus in *Histoire(s) du Cinéma* he undermines the literal contemporaneity of the cinema screen by drawing up its archeological depths and showing how each cinematic icon is both a memory and reinvention of earlier imagery and events. Godard, watching his memory on screen, undergoes and conveys to the audience a moment of historical stillness in a fulcrum of impinging icons that have colonized our private and public lives.

Tornatore's *Cinema Paradiso* (1989), resituates the cultural memory of cinematic perception in the peripheries of European modernity. In his depiction of cinema-going in a post-war Sicilian town, viewing the movies entails an outpouring of emotions and stories as the audience speaks to, carries on dialogues with, and co-narrates the on-screen action. These scenes hark back to Buck-Morss's description of early turn-of-the century cinema and to the possibility that it was not only perceptual naiveté that caused audiences to flee oncoming on-screen locomotives. In Tornatore's film, the everyday life of the Sicilian audience is articulated with the on-screen imagery shown, and even replaces it, as the townspeople actively retool cinema into organ of their own social memory.

For Buck-Morss, one such modern receptacle of social memory is the empowering rhetoric of the mass or the collective, which she posits as the joint fabrication of cinematic and political discourse. The imagery of the crowd compensates for and resynthesizes the fragmentation of individual experience in modernity, and is the site where individuals can recover and participate in the life-world of public memory. Yet the crowd-mass, for Buck-Morss, citing the work of Eisenstein, is a visual fabrication that can only be seen in and as totality on the cinema screen. As pure cinematic object, it subtends and materializes the tenuous reality of the masses in everyday life. Feldman asks the same questions of the post-colonial bodies of Iraqis and African-Americans: to what extent is the experience and ideological construction of the social body contingent on technological prosthetics applied to the individual body? And to what extent does this enhancing and even surrealizing of the sensory apparatus of the viewer eviscerate and empty the sensory pertinence and subjectivity of the viewed?

Feldman's essay underscores and advances Buck-Morss's crucial point that visual prosthesis not only envisioned the mass with a new powerful synthesis but that the act of viewing itself provided a new "mass experience," a new way to participate in society and history. Feldman shows how this creation and mobilization of a collective through technological prosthetics can manufacture consent for war or can collectivize in a traumatic fashion previously inadmissible experience such as the initial shock of a black man's beating. Both affects, acquiescence and shock, can be rapidly undermined by the very disposability of such imagery. The phenomena of media disposability here raises the even more haunting issues of the disposability of the collective that is momentarily gathered together and then disbanded by changing the mobilizing imagery and channels of perception. What effect does this momentary synchronic crowd have on the perception of history? What other kinds of acuity can survive and persevere through the orchestration of intermittent collective experience and affect?

Eventually both Feldman and Buck-Morss settle on the function of pain in cinematic modernity. Though they appear to speak only of visual realities, their concern is the distillation of bodily experience by optical metaphors; they are the sieve through which other sensory realities are passed, gleaned and discarded. For Buck-Morss, the crowd in the theater is enervated by optical pain to the same extent that the stars on the screen become anaesthetized bodies with each visual engrossment of the actors' physical presence. American cinema fabricates the individual star as a mass and Russian cinema fabricates the mass, the collective, as a singularity. Both interventions entail cultural constructions of the body. These diverse acts of embodiment carry with them an inheritance of the senses that we have not yet come to terms with. In Feldman's essay too, the perceptual reality of the courtroom jury is elaborately constructed through the evisceration of the bodily subjectivity of Rodney King. King's body

becomes monumental as both a racial and legal object in direct propor-
tion to the silencing of his pain.

*   *   *

Frykman re-assesses everyday life not as the after-effect of power relations originating outside the everyday sphere, but rather as a privileged
site for the constitution of somatic identity that is ultimately nationalized. This implies a personification of sensorial experience that runs
counter to the truth claims of the public sphere. In Sweden, in the first
half of this century, the private sphere, one of the most typifying inven-
tions of modern experience, is also the zone where the transitoriness, in-
securities and instabilities of modern life are evaded in the search for
continuity and identity. Because this search aggravates a bifurcation between public and private experience, it has an impact on the formation of
sensory memory. The bracketing of private and subjective sensory trauma emanating from encounters with the public sphere denudes everyday
life of any conscious political and historical salience. Frykman traces the
convergence, in early Swedish modernity, between private experience,
sensory rehabilitation, and the modern concept of "nature." A triangle
that Swedes institutionalize, through a variety of social practices, as a
privileged zone of authenticity and pre-social truth. This perceptual rehabilitation of everyday life-worlds and populist reform of the body, the
senses and private life occurs via an anti-modernist search for ahistorical
certainty in nature. Frykman notes an important repositioning of nature
from pre-modern to modern Sweden. Nature, in the pre-modern, was an
extension of socio-economic peasant activity, oral culture and rules of inheritance; it was a collectivized and social terrain. By this century, the
discursive and material relation to nature had migrated to the sphere of
private experience where it serves as a compensation for the encroach-
ments of urban life.

Nature, sensory experience, and physical culture, though cultivated in
the private sphere, are meant to instill an extra-individual certainty to the
structure of experience as opposed to pushing experience to more extreme forms of subjectivity. Physical culture and the recreational wilderness emerge as collective templates of experience, that, despite their
pre-political aura, become building blocks of national identity. Frykman
also shows that to the same extent that Swedes were pursuing sensory
truth in the private sphere, the private sphere was the object of rationalization by the public domain. In the inter-war period, the Swedish
kitchen was both reformed and colonized by having been turned into a
diminutive replica of the sanitary scientific laboratory. The sterilized
kitchen became the meta-embodiment of modern Swedish women, equal

in its improvements to the somatic rationality of gymnastics. The modernization of the Swedish kitchen speaks to how social identity was altered through the re-organization of the domestic sensorium and its commensal codes. The current intervention on commensal content and practices undertaken by EEC today can be seen as an indirect heir of these Swedish reforms.

Frykman, like Buck-Morss, demonstrates how the relation between the self and the senses, as much as it appears particular, is not a matter for private life alone. Reorganizing the self's relation to perception can also create the mass, the collective. Thus exercise, gymnastics, and the recreational consumption of nature, undertaken in the pursuit of individual pleasure, become the experience, performance, and public visualization of mass identity. So, as in Buck-Morss's description of early cinema viewing, the Swedish co-rehabilitation of body and nature becomes a vast experiment in social mimesis.

The Senses and Recent Perspectives
on Material Culture

Many current studies of material culture and commensality in cultural anthropology focus on classificatory analysis of objects and substances and their diverse uses. My interest in discussing these approaches is not to survey the field, but to connect and to apply the senses to exemplary domains, thereby drawing implications for wider anthropological theory. Can an anthropology of the senses uncover new convergences between diverse specializations, such as commensal studies, analyses of material artifacts and cultures, exchange practices, cognitive theory, social agency theory, and the anthropology of history?

Classification analysis of material culture is prominent in several important and recent works. Mary Douglas's (1991) central concern for instance in the study of alcohol and other comestibles is the "quantity and incidence of rules" that govern consumption which can offer up "a sociology of sociability." Douglas focuses on the extent to which the discrimination of substances in acts of consumption stand for the discrimination of social statuses. The material artifact functions as a stage upon which social structure can be played out. Douglas argues for the analysis of comestibles because the analyst of commensality addresses a "world of things" and pragmatic acts, rather than conceptual abstractions. But she offers no account on *how* a "world" of things is perceptually constituted and become emblematic of social structure, nor on the sensory interplay between meaning and substance which actively embodies social categories and biography in food. Rather, in commensal events the social subject functions as mere go-between, a conduit that connects social codes and the substances upon which they are meant to be displayed. By valorizing rules and discriminations that circulate and stratify things, substances and persons, Douglas precludes a genealogy of sensory practice and object formation. She abstracts from things a finished societal mind whose rules are writ large on socialized substance. Here substance has no cultural or analytic status, until it is inserted into pre-existing protocols of distribution and consumption. The stratigraphic object, as the embodiment of historical experience and as exceeding its instrumental profile, is ignored in favor of synchronic norms of *ceremonial utility*. As pointed out in chapter 1, this flattening of substance into synchronic categories of inclusion/exclusion cannot accommodate the notion of alcohol, food and other material as the bearers of histories of commensal events and codes. Yet, it is through the stories that are borne in objects and substances that a community narrates itself in an open-ended fashion that cannot be reduced to a pre-arranged structuralist game plan.

Weiner and Schneider (1988) also speak of material artifacts, especially cloth, as capturing and passing down official classification systems in time and space. In their introduction to *Cloth and Human Experience*, they approach cloth, as a surface where collective norms, values and codes are deposited by social institutions and subsequently recovered for ideological mobilization(1988: 1–29). They recognize that the chromatic, textural and aromatic qualities of cloth achieve cultural and collective significance in various societies. However, they bypass the sphere of sensory action and reception by emphasizing two poles of social effect: the origins of codes in social institutions and their terminus in cloth as a collective text. Labor, design practices, the preparation of materials and relations of production are treated as disembodied instruments that transfer by rote, cultural codes from institution to object. Cloth, like Althusser's social subject, is posited as a support of larger social institutions. Passing down cloth artifacts and cloth making traditions, such as ceremonial banners and clothing, is the mechanical creation of an institutional memory which frequently suppresses the crevices and contradictions of everyday experience in favor of large scale and socially binding, myths and icons.

In this social coding of cloth, the senses either as agents, subject and object of inscription and reception are implicitly reduced to culturally vacant instruments. Although Schneider and Weiner note the classificatory connections of the body, sexuality, female reproduction and death, and the making of cloth artifacts, the body as a material actor and mediator is eliminated from their analysis. This gap generates an automaton model of cognition where the transparent meanings of society are teleported to the clairvoyant surfaces of cloth which then deliver these codes to the minds of social actors.

Cloth, despite all its possible multi-cultural and sensorial densities, becomes as transparent as the absent senses; the artifact becomes an easily glimpsed mirror for the exposure of social ideology. Such shadow play between institutional surface and the object's cognitive surface, is rooted in a *photo-centric* model of cognition. There is a mimetic correspondence between the theorists' reading of cloth as text and their implicit model of the circulation of social values and codes as if they were rays of light. Their optical model requires no excavation, no mediating and interruptive textures of the thing or the senses, and no emotional force; only the transparency and facileness of ideology and object as mutually reflecting mirrors and the hidden amenities of vision.

To what extent does the reading-text metaphor, when used to decode multi-sensory artifacts like cloth, skew interpretation by silencing indigenous modes of sensory investment and reception (Ong 1982)? In those societies where cloth was so heavily invested with social meaning, history, emotion and remembrance, what other modes of perception were in play? How did they touch cloth and what did they touch through it?

What happens to the senses when theorists haul meaning from social institutions to material artifacts and then back again *as if the dense and embodied communication between persons and things were only a quick exchange between surfaces?*

*   *   *

An anthropology of the senses, as elaborated in this volume is concerned with how intrinsic perceptual qualities of objects express their sensory history, and how this salience can motivate and animate their exchange and shared consumption. Broad ranging and reductive classifications of material culture can suppress this dimension in favor of synchronic and functional descriptions of rules and categories of property, transmission, exchange and consumption. In turn, the depiction of objects as passive refractions of pre-existing ideational social codes and norms tends to accommodate only those social narratives that are residual, official and institutional.

Nicholas Thomas (1991), in his social history of exchange theories and material culture, also recognizes the deficit in the wholesale homogenizing of objects via reductive systems of classification such as prestation rules. His book, *Entangled Objects,* contains brief but fascinating discussions of the perceptual-visual dynamics in the European appropriation-depiction of indigenous objects. Yet Thomas holds onto a crucial classificatory polarity that is of concern to the anthropology of the senses in material culture. He theoretically devalues the "personal" estimation of an object, the "idiosyncratic" self-object relation, in favor of the "systemic" circulation of commodities and gifts (1991:21–22, 30–31). For Thomas the distinction between the "idiosyncratic" and the "systemic dynamics of [object] transactions" is largely one of social classification and of limited versus general semantic gauges. This is based partly on his separating the emotive from the political dimension of material culture and prestation and his dismissing of the affective as less socially relevant (1991:7). In contrast, sensory analyses in this volume endeavors to show how the difference between the apparently idiosyncratic and the systemic in a material culture is not only a matter of classification and utility but may well embody a profound political and historical divergence.

Within a society that is undergoing turbulent shifts in material values, modes of representation, and systems of reference, there can be a systemic character to the idiosyncratic which frequently only registers at the level of the senses. I can also suggest that an anthropology of the senses would show how the instrumental dichotomy between systemic and idiosyncratic valuation in material culture can be the political polarity between the valued and the devalued, between public-institutional memory and unspeakable memories of cultural alterity. This polarity emanates from the ideological closure of dominant institutional and cultural canons that can desocialize, among other things, dissonant consumption practices, popular aesthetics and artistic genres, divergent sexual practices, unacceptable fetishism, and subaltern identities. The apparently "idiosyncratic" investment in objects and substances may be the tip of a submerged social language of materiality that has not achieved formal legitimation, but which may have a firmer grasp on the mutable structure of experience in which all things undergo recontextualization into novel and as yet unnarrated constellations.

Recontextualization is one of the primary concerns for Appadurai (1986) when he speaks of the life-history or social biography of the object, and how it can pass in and out of diverse regimes of valuation. This can imply that the object can be jettisoned from the systemic into the idiosyncratic and subsequently rehabilitated as a socially pertinent article. Yet, Appadurai does not examine the impact of recontextualized objects on sensory deformation and social agency. For his primary interest in the different and discontinuous phases of the object's life history is the extent to which these mutations throw up diverse analytic profiles for the theorist. He does not explore how this non-identity of the object with itself in its accumulated social biography affects the situated social memories and identities of persons that were carried and discarded along with the artifact as it undergoes revaluation. To look at the life history of the signifying object from this side is to begin to access indigenous cultural constructions of history that are recoverable from the created material world; it is also to encounter how history is made in the present through the semantic potentials of material artifacts and relations.

*   *   *

The relationship between public culture, institutional memory and the hierarchical selection of system-supporting objects is also a central concern of Weiner's recent book *Inalienable Possessions* (1992). She divides material culture into two classes: movables and immovables, what is given-exchanged and what is kept. Maussian exchange theories are seen as inadequate because they ignore the cultural desire to hold on to, and not give away objects which support social identity, hegemony and power in time and space. She calls this identity-endowing capacity of usually aged articles, cosmological authentication and makes universal claims for this framework beyond Melanesia.

Given their genealogy, and institutional position, such authoritative artifacts can sanction experiences and cultural identities in a selective and ultimately political fashion. Therefore any act or artifact of authentication also carries with it an opposite effect of de-authentication, or a denial of authority and value, that seeks to de-legitimize experiences, identities and other objects (such as those that are given away in exchange cycles). Weiner goes only so far as to elaborate on the status-creating import of authenticating artifacts and acts. But an exploration of what is left over from acts and objects of authentication would encounter zones of inadmissible experience, memory, and identity that invariably fall out of any discrimination that divides the valued from valueless, meaning from non-meaning and power from that which lacks power.

Such boundary creating acts and objects, and the historical impact of what they discard and exclude, entail sensorial, perceptual and memory effects that the authors in this book have repeatedly discussed. They would agree with Weiner that the material world is a depth from which salient social identities can be made, unmade, recreated and passed on. At the same time, the essays by Feldman, Frykman and myself show that the fundamental disordering, institutional repression and perceptual discrediting of material experience can diminish the narrative efficacy of material culture and block the historical poetics of identity and memory.

Crucial to any process of authentication is the moment when certain objects are selected over others as sites of social anchorage. This results in the discarding and marginalization of sensory values, meaning and emotions attached to discredited materialities. Acts and artifacts of authentication do not only generate differentiating social statuses, as Weiner states, but also emerge from the context of status conflicts, that is, from a political environment and from asymmetric relations of power. Existing authenticities can be pitted against the desire of marginals and subalterns to authenticate, through material culture, what has been denied representation, and which invariably harbors alternative sensory postures (Seremetakis 1991; Feldman 1991). For Weiner these residues are simply "fragmentary" and inherently anti-social. The possibility that things, acts and actors are *unequally authentic* in any society renders Weiner's renewal of referentiality, of the inalienable, in culture *and* in cultural studies, problematic.

The need for an anthropology of the senses and an accompanying theory of reception at this point suggests that possessiveness and status-drives alone, cannot explain how the sheer literality of an object's power is created; how things become essentialized, and how they make history real in the absence of direct experience of the past. Without an examination of perception, beyond that of ideational reflection theory, we can only talk of how a Cartesian 'ego' possesses and keeps objects; but we cannot talk of how and why embodied agents become possessed by the object as a historical fetish. Taussig's (1993) discussion of the mimetic[1] relationships between the material culture of the colonized and the colonizing addresses precisely this dynamic of possession, as it relates to authenticating objects, as does Stoller's (1992) analysis of the ethnography of Jean Rouch. Another example is Herzfeld's (1991) study of conflicting kin and state claims to folk architecture in Crete, which traces the performative dynamics of contesting authenticities and unequal inalienable artifacts. However Herzfeld, sees the "history" offered by the authenticating artifact (old houses), as a rhetoric that promotes underlying synchronic oppositions. Thus, like Weiner, he reduces the historicity of a material culture to a utility that is manipulated in a Hobbsean competition for status and scarce resources.

For Weiner, to historicize an object means that engaged social actors become incarcerated in the cultural authority and allure of the past, unable to encode the present except passively through the lens of what has already occurred. Or can we ask: is even the most hoary authenticating object, ultimately, yet incompletely, torn from its past by the gaze and touch of the present? Furthermore, an exclusive focus on cosmological authentication *cannot* account for the stratigraphic witness of the artifact, when history and perceptual experience renders the artifact nonidentical to itself. Yet this book suggests that it is this layered non-identity, and not monosemic authenticity, that captures the winding sensory passage of historicity through the forest of things.

The lens of monosemic authenticity gravitates to dominant cultural codes and to the sanctioned reproduction of public memory and culture. Thus Weiner deploys "classical" Melanesian culture(s) as an inalienable anthropological object which confers authentication on her theoretical frameworks for which she argues a much more global gauge. When she exports this perspective to non-Melanesian contexts, *Greece* is strategically chosen as *another inalienable artifact*. Weiner selects archaic Greece and does so without remarking how this culture and its iconography have traditionally functioned as an authenticating capital within western sensibility, politics and knowledge. Of relevance to Weiner is sculpture like Venus (Aphrodite) whose cosmic inalienability is confirmed by its very passage from religious artifact to an aestheticized treasure (1992:42). At this point one must ask from what perceptual and sensory site does Weiner speak when she declares such a culture-traversing artifact as transcendentally authenticating? Does not this global transcendental affirmation emanate from the "non-situated" and panoptic position of the classical western theorist?

*   *   *

In this model of cosmological authentication there is no substantive perceptual and emotional difference between the artifact sanctified in an identity-producing ritual and the artifact ensconced in a museum display case. In both contexts the object is an authenticating permanence. Weiner offers no analysis of divergent and culturally mediated perceptual affects. The historical transfer of authenticity simply happens because it emanates from the old object. Both the ritual and museum object are related aspects of a singular referential power that attests to the object's essentialized immutable inalienability in time and space. Therefore the exclusive perspective of cosmological authentication not only suppresses perceptual asymmetries within particular cultural formations but between them as well.

The Inalienable State

The recent finds in Vergina, Greece, made by the archaeologist Manolis Andronikos, uncovered the tombs of Macedonian royalty including the remains of Philip II. Vergina was a sacred, politico-religious site of the Macedonian kingdom. Recent events in the Balkans, particularly the claiming of the name "Macedonia" by the newly formed republic at Skopia, rapidly transformed Vergina into a contemporary political symbol, or what Harvey (1989) calls an imaginary space of representation.

The politicization of the Vergina finds was exemplified by the appropriation of the Macedonian star—an emblem found at Vergina—as a national symbol by the Skopian government. Both governments, at Skopia and Athens, deployed Vergina to authenticate their respective territorial claims based on inalienable Macedonian and Greek identities. The archaeological and the archaic were used to blur the modern origins of both states in order to fabricate a chronological legitimacy that reached back beyond modernity into antiquity. Here archaeological remains became crucial components of the material culture of the state. All of this undoubtedly supports Weiner's thesis of inalienable authenticating objects. However, does this appropriation of the Vergina finds by the state as inalienable capital exhaust their cultural reception and representation in the Greek context? Let us listen to Andronikos, the discoverer of Vergina.

On the Native Point of View

For Andronikos, archaeology

as a historical discipline works, like all episteme, with abstract schemata, general concepts, and aims at conceiving the general laws and rules that regulate human life ... Yet the archaeologist in his research encounters concrete objects, creations of a particular, known or unknown, creator, which were used by some human being ... He finds epigraphs referring to concrete people or discovers the grave of a man, a woman or child; he knows that in the ruins of a house once lived a family, rich or poor, which left us the remains of its everyday life. We touch almost always with our fingers the touch of, not the unknown or non-existing king Asinis, but the existential person, with his joys and sorrows, hopes and pains ... If ... we approach in a humane way—poetically we could say—some monuments of the past, if instead of classifying them in the cold schemata of our conceptual constructions, we see them or read them as images and voices of a human existence which sees us and talks to us from the depths of centuries, we could perhaps gain much more "data" to help contemporary human beings, ourselves, to feel less lonely and lost in the chaos of centuries and perpetual flow of innumerable humans ... Some concrete examples: ... According to Herodotus, [Greek soldiers who marched with the Egyptian army to Abu Simbel in 591 BC] ... there at the feet of the colossus they inscribed their names ... Each one with his burning pain (*kaimós*) in life, but also his pride, they are no longer the anonymous mass that histories refer to. Each one has a name and homeland and wants to inscribe them on the stone not to be forgotten ... This human dimension of the epigraphic witness, only the poet can transfer to us convincingly, as Cavafy has done in his poem "*En to mini Athyr.*"

If we stand in front of a prosthesis of the museum of Olympia, [we will see] a helmet ... simply named Miltiades ... Who would need further identification to recognize Miltiades's helmet that he wore in the battle of Marathon? That unique finding which has no place in the written history nor in the history of art or technology, constitutes alone the most exciting witness of the famous battle, equal to the Aeschylean verses on another event ... There are times that the archaeological object equals the dense poetic logos and expresses the otherwise unspeakable, that which lays deep in the human soul ... (Andronikos 1988)

The classical world, especially the ancient Greek world, stands in front of everyone, in every epoch, as a fully-living problem. For its solution, every human being will start from his own problems that he struggles to embrace in order to give them the answer our life demands. The classical

world stands still, unchanging in front of the researchers. It is they who
move and change position and stance towards it, pumping out [meaning]
endlessly from it which remains inexhaustible like the sea. (From Andronikos's first book [1951] in Christides 1993)

For Andronikos then, archaeology is not just an objectification of material culture as "abstract schemata," "general concepts," "rules," or the
fetishization of monuments. The practice of archaeology has its own material culture. He turns to tactile dialogue. Classificatory frameworks objectify a finding as "the king of Asinis" but the perceptual dynamics of
excavation involve "a touch . . . with our fingers" of "the touch of the
existential person with his joys and sorrows, hopes and pains." The two
existential tactilities, the senses, meet and exchange through the centuries via the object. Thus we must "read" the finds, with the eyes and
hands "as images and voices of a human existence which sees us and
talks to us from the depths of centuries . . ." Andronikos here speaks to
the sensory and perceptual reception of the archaeological artifact as an
"epigraphic witness." Witnessing is a dialogical process and exchange
between the fieldworker and the artifact. It is an exchange of non-
contemporary existentials, between the archaeologist and the absent
other whom the artifact witnesses. For Andronikos the encounter of existentials is that "unique finding" that cannot be situated in written history,
the history of arts or technology. It has no place in the "cold schemata
of our conceptual constructions." It simply belongs to the "dense poetic
logos" that expresses the "unspeakable."
      The exchange of sensory and emotional existentials between the ex-
cavator and the excavated is not merely a psychological moment, for
Andronikos. It speaks to a particular epistemological and political relation between the present and the past. He speaks of witnessing as perceptual, emotional and moral process. The archaeological find and material
culture "stands in front of everyone in every epoch as a fully living
problem. For its solution, every human being will start from his own
problems that he struggles to embrace and give them the answer our life
demands."
      Here Andronikos explicitly challenges the fixity of the authenticating
artifact as an arbitrary inheritance, and as imposed code from the past.
The past is as unavoidable as the sea. He looks at the existential structure
of the present, its shifting positions, as mediating and animating the perception of history to the extent that the past is "endlessly pumping out"
meanings and consequences for the present. As I have stated earlier, the
semantic depth of the material artifact, its historicity, is contingent on
the ongoing shifts and displacement of the perceptual structure of the
present which continuously offers new prospects on the past, new memories, and new experiences of historical memory itself. *The archaeological*

object, in its widest sense, acquires another and new stratigraphic level each time it enters into the perceptual order of the present.

Thus the encounter with the possibly authenticating artifact proceeds through a multiplex series of exchanges. There is the exchange between the "excavator" and the everyday life of society; there is the exchange generated by the conveyance of this accumulated experience to the "archaeological site" as a special space of perception where sensory and emotional reciprocities between the present and the past occur. Through this sedimentation of exchanges excavation, in the widest sense of the term, becomes an identity-transforming performance; one that creates both subjects and objects, in the very process of fieldwork.

* * *

By looking once again at these stones, I remember that I spent a whole life here. I came young, 17 years old. That's how it always happens with excavation. Excavating research, like any scholarly research, wants persistence, patience, and no hurry. You may have to wait for years. It demands devotion and desire. It is not something programmed. You work and suddenly you gain something, a knowledge. You discover a beautiful finding that gives you satisfaction because first you succeeded in your work and then because you offered to others. I see all the people coming to admire these ruins and I say to myself that I offered something. I made it possible for others to enjoy and gain from what I gained.

[When a discovery at Vergina was made in November 1977]

We saw something it was impossible for me to imagine for never to that moment such an ossuary had been found: an all-golden larnax with an impressive, engraved star on its cover. We took it out of the sarcophagus, I placed it on the ground and opened it. Everyone's eyes opened widely and our breath "was cut": the burnt bones, well cleaned and placed in a carefully formed pile, still retained the color from the cloth that once folded them in ... We felt the need to get back up to light, to breath fresh air. When I got out, I distanced myself from my co-workers, visitors, police, and stood alone for a moment, to recover from the unbelievable view. Everything showed we had found a royal tomb; and if the dating was correct, I could not dare think about it. For the first time I felt a strong chill, something like an electric current along my spinal cord. So, if the date was correct, if these were royal remains, then I had held in my hands the bones of Philip? It was frightening, impossible for the mind to bear. That night it was impossible for me to sleep. It was the most unbelievable hour of my life .... I decided it was wise to speak to no one [about it] ...

[After the completion of several excavations]

I got up in the morning to go to the university to announce the results of the excavation ... Only when I entered the amphitheater of the old building, where I once took my first lessons, I came back in touch with reality. And then I understood that what we had done in the solitude of Vergina did not concern only us, the archaeologists ... Today I know that no satisfaction and no honor can be compared to the love of the people who told me "thank you for what you gave us. Be well and strong!" (Excerpts, from Andronikos's book *Vergina*, that appeared in the newspaper *Ta Nea* on March 31, 1992, the day of his death)

These statements of Andronikos are not merely stereotypical biographical reminiscences of the scientist stepping back from the rigors of rationalism. They also speak to his perceptual process and sensory dislocation in the field, that is his moment of historical stillness, when past and present, the ground upon which he walked, and the hollow excavated caverns beneath him, were held in suspension in order to achieve a new balance, a new historical relation. At that moment of stillness his own world was defamiliarized in a fieldwork experience as profound as any ethnographic journey should be.

*   *   *

Reading Andronikos's accounts, long after having written an ethnography of death in Greece, I was struck by the extent to which his descriptions spontaneously echoed discourses of the women of Inner Mani, the other end of Greece from Macedonia. These women of the Southern Peloponnese, like Andronikos, exhume the bones of the dead and practice the material poetics of the past.

Andronikos speaks of both the excavator and the excavated as "witnesses." Women of the Southern Peloponnese, who mourn and wake the dead (at burials and exhumation) also use the expression "to witness" someone (*na ton martyrísoume*) meaning "to witness, suffer for, and to reveal the truth about the dead ... To witness, to suffer for, and to come out as representative for, are narrative devices in laments that fuse jural notions of reciprocity and truth-claiming with the emotional nuances of pain" (Seremetakis 1991:102).

Witnessing is both a fully embodied performance and an active intervention within the mourning ritual by which the experience and emotions of the mourner and their estimation of the dead and their material remains, achieve authentication and authority. It is a form of truth-claiming with the body and bones of the deceased that requires mourners to exchange emotions, discourse and pains in their fullest sensory and emotional force.

*   *   *

When Andronikos opens the imputed tomb of Phillip II: "Everyone's eyes opened widely ... : the burnt bones, well cleaned and placed in a carefully formed pile, still retained the color from the robe in which they once were folded." And in another excavation, a Maniat woman recounts:

> "... I went down three meters deep I opened the *kivotó* [the coffin] and found the corpse *unrecognizable.* I sat and with the smallest detail gathered even the last little bone, even a little tooth on the jaw. The clothes and everything [including the bones] *were burnt from the humidity and the time* ..."
> (Seremetakis 1991: 184)

The buried bones Andronikos uncovered were burnt by ritual cremation. This is not the case for the Maniat exhumers. For them the "burnt" bones is a visual-tactile and even aromatic reception of the materially transformative passage of the artifact in time. The sense of the grave's contents being "burnt" by time historicizes the bones from the perceptual angle of the present. Burning, adds another stratigraphic layer to the artifact. Burning is the solidification of the senses of the exhumer onto the affective object. A crucial component of witnessing the dead, their artifacts and through these, the past, is witnessing, with the senses and emotions, the material alterity of time on the bones and personal possessions of the dead.

From my own analysis of the allegorical significance of "burnt" bones:

> The scattered residue of the grave opened for exhumation, is described ... as "burnt by humidity and time." In another narrative the rotten, damp shards of the wooden coffin are likened to "ashes" ... In exhumation, temporal transformation, the tense relation between the past and present, divides the body into the decaying and desiccated, flesh and bones ... The exhumer, by collecting and ordering the bones, creates the "second body" of the dead. The juxtaposition between the rotting and the desiccated, the past and the present, does not cause the mourner to abandon the remains as depersonalized inert artifacts but compels her to enter into a new symbolic-material relation with the dead." (Seremetakis 1991: 187–189)

Exhumation is *a ceremony of authentication* in which the bones of the ancestor are validated as *an inalienable artifact* of the kin group, particularly the women mourners, through performances of purification (cleaning the bones) and reassemblage; performances that mold the bones as historical substance. However, in contrast to Weiner's (1992) understanding of authentication as purely a cognitive, Hobbsean and agonistic differentiation of social status, the Maniat exhumation rite authenticates because it addresses the alienability of the past and the ancestor and touches history and estrangement as pain (*pónos*) made palpable by the artifact frayed by time:

The preparation of the corpse before the burial and, later, the cleaning and ordering of the bones construct the dead as an effigy, as a "doll" (*skoútsa*). Adornment and ornamentation, cleaning, ordering, divination, and narration of the bones generate tangible emotions. The clean bones are tangible memory, a fossil held in the palm. In life and death, the self is "dressed" with the eye of others. The self is dressed with eyes, memory, and language. Emotions are tangible because the senses of the body are the templates of feeling. To remember and to adorn is to embody emotions. The embodiment of feeling is shared substance. Shared substance is not merely the sharing of objects but rather the exchange of artifacts of emotions. The tending of exhumed bones revolves around the issue of who does it. This performance must be based on shared substance with the dead. That is why there were never paid mourners in Inner Mani: paid mourning does not require shared substance as an exchange of emotions. *Tears shed without a common history of reciprocity are matter out of place.* The shared artifact historicizes exchanges of feeling. It is a treasure kept and revered (*filahtó*) and acquires a sacred quality. This is especially so when the artifact stands for a person absent by death or journey. The view of such artifacts by the recipient provokes an immediate response: tears. Tangible emotions. There is an exchange of artifacts at moments of separation. That is why at exhumation the sight of bones inspires lamentation, often as intense as the first *kláma*. Bones at exhumation become tangible emotive substitutes of the absent flesh. (Seremetakis 1991: 215–16)

*   *   *

"Burning" is the perceptual affect of time and memory on the object and the exhumer. It is the defamiliarizing meeting with the discards of the other, that is "our" past. The "native archaeologist" relives, at the level of perception and feeling, the journey made by the exhumed object into the present. The artifact, as the "epigraphic witness" of the absent other, is feeling solidified and historicized. For the object brought forth from the depths of forgetfulness and history burns with the memory of the senses.

Notes

1. However Taussig's notion of mimesis emphasizes an idealized moment of first and primal "sensuous contact" which gives rise to subsequent mimetic play. This model tends to treat the mimetic (that which happens after first contact) primarily as a cognitive process which has a preliminary, but less important, material side. At the same time the focus on first sensuous contact as the precondition of mimesis or what I call re-perception, seems to drift towards a reductive materialism.

References

Andronikos, Manolis. 1988. "The Human Side of Archaeology." *To Vema,* 12/18/88.

———. 1992. *Vergina: The Royal Tombs.* Athens: Ekdotike Athenon.

Appadurai, Arjun, ed. 1986. *The Social Life of Things: Commodities in Cultural Perspective.* Cambridge: Cambridge University Press.

Corbin, Alain. 1986. *The Foul and the Fragrant: Odor and the French Social Imagination.* New York: Berg Publishers.

Crary, Jonathan. 1991. *Techniques of the Observer: On Vision and Modernity in the Nineteenth Century.* Cambridge, Mass: MIT Press.

Christides, T. 1993. "The Teacher." *To Vema,* March 28, 1993.

Douglas, Mary, ed. 1991. *Constructive Drinking: Perspectives on Drink from Anthropology.* Cambridge: Cambridge University Press.

Harvey, David. 1989. *The Condition of Postmodernity: An Inquiry into the Origins of Cultural Change.* Oxford: Blackwell.

Herzfeld, Michael. 1991. *A Place in History: Social and Monumental Time in a Cretan Town.* Princeton: Princeton University Press.

Howes, David, ed. 1991. *The Varieties of Sensory Experience.* Toronto: University of Toronto Press.

Husserl, Edmund. 1964. *The Idea of Phenomenology.* Trans. W. Alston & G. Nakhnikian. The Hague: Martinus Nijhoff.

Jameson, Fredric. 1981. *The Political Unconscious: Narrative as a Socially Symbolic Act.* Ithaca: Cornell University Press.

Ong, Walter J. 1982. *Orality and Literacy.* New York: Methuen.

Seremetakis, C. Nadia. 1991. *The Last Word: Women, Death and Divination in Inner Mani.* Chicago: University of Chicago Press.

Stoller, Paul. 1992. *The Cinematic Griot: The Ethnography of Jean Rouch.* Chicago: University of Chicago Press.

Taussig, Michael. 1993. *Mimesis and Alterity: A Particular History of the Senses.* New York: Routledge.

Thomas, Nicholas. 1991. *Entangled Objects: Exchange, Material Culture, and Capitalism in the Pacific.* Cambridge, Mass: Harvard University Press.

Tyler, Stephen A. 1987. *The Unspeakable: Discourse, Dialogue, and Rhetoric in the Postmodern World.* Madison: University of Wisconsin Press.

Weiner, Annette. 1992. *Inalienable Possessions: The Paradox of Keeping-While-Giving.* Berkeley: University of California Press.

Weiner, Annette & Jane Schneider, eds. 1989. *Cloth and Human Experience.* Washington: Smithsonian Institution Press.

Films Cited

Godard, Jean-Luc. 1989. *Histoire(s) du Cinéma.* JLG Films.

Tornatore, Giuseppe. 1989. *Cinema Paradiso.* Miramax Films.

About the Contributors

Susan Buck-Morss is the author of *The Dialectics of Seeing: Walter Benjamin and the Arcades Project* (MIT Press 1989) and *The Origin of Negative Dialectics: Theodore W. Adorno, Walter Benjamin and the Frankfurt Institute* (Free Press 1979). She is Professor of Philosophy and Social Theory at Cornell University, and she is currently engaged with field and archival research on political culture and modernity in the former Soviet Union.

Allen Feldman is the author of *Formations of Violence: the Narrative of the Body and Political Terror in Northern Ireland* (University of Chicago Press 1991), *The Northern Fiddler* (Blackstaff Press 1985), and *Towards a Political Anthropology of the Body* (Westview Press, forthcoming). He is Director of Ethnographic Evaluation at the Center for AIDS Outreach and Prevention, New York, and has been visiting professor of Anthropology in the Department of Performance Studies in New York University, The Institute for Critical Studies in the New School for Social Research, and the University of Lund, Sweden.

Jonas Frykman is the co-author of *Culture Builders: A Historical Anthropology of Middle-Class Life* (Rutgers University Press 1987). He is also the author of numerous articles in European ethnological and folklore journals and of a forthcoming book on modern Swedish intelligentsia. He is the co-founder of what is known as the "Lund school" of Swedish historical anthropology and is Professor of Ethnology and Folklore at the University of Bergen, Norway.

C. Nadia Seremetakis is author of *The Last Word: Women, Death and Divination in Inner Mani* (The University of Chicago Press, 1991), which won the Victor Turner award in 1992, and editor of *Ritual, Power, and Body* (Pella, 1993). She has written numerous articles in European and American scholarly journals and has held appointments at Vassar College, New York University, and the National School of Public Health in Athens. Currently working on recent immigrant populations in Greece and related issues of transnational health and disease, she is Advisor to the Minister at the Ministry of Health in Greece.

Paul Stoller is the author of *The Cinematic Griot: The Ethnography of Jean Rouch* (University of Chicago Press 1992), *Fusion of the Worlds: An Ethnography of Possession among the Songhay of Niger* (University of Chicago Press 1989), *The Taste of Ethnographic Things: The Senses in Anthropology* (University of Pennsylvania Press 1989), and of numerous articles. He is Professor of Anthropology at West Chester University.